RECOVERY AT WORK

RECOVERY AT WORK

A Clean and Sober Career Guide

Carol Cox Smith, M.A. Ed.

With a Foreword by James M. Schaefer, Ph.D.

1817

A Hazelden Book

Harper & Row, Publishers, San Francisco

New York, Grand Rapids, Philadelphia, St. Louis
London, Singapore, Sydney, Tokyo, Toronto

FIRST HARPER & ROW EDITION PUBLISHED IN 1990.

Library of Congress Cataloging-in-Publication Data

Smith, Carol Cox.
    Recovery at work : a clean and sober career guide / Carol Cox Smith.
      p.   cm.
    "A Hazelden book."
    ISBN 0–06–255382–8
    1. Drugs and employment. 2. Alcohol and employment.
3. Vocational guidance. I. Title.
HF5549.5.D7S65 1990   89–45994
362.29′186 — dc20   CIP

---

90 91 92 93 94 BANTA 10 9 8 7 6 5 4 3 2 1

To the three people who know me best and help me most:

Al
Dodie
Florence

CONTENTS

FOREWORD

It's been said that the most effective way to cope with change is to help create it. Well, here's the guidebook for people who are in the process of getting on with their careers after having faced problems with alcohol and other drugs.

Recovery at Work by Carol Cox Smith has important and readable advice on recovery from chemical dependency in corporate America. For many years, people have returned to their jobs after going through treatment for chemical dependency. This is a book on a problem that has certainly been neglected by many of their co-workers and bosses.

Chemical dependency counselors, social workers, treatment staff, families, employee assistance staff, co-workers, company supervisors, and bosses have failed to recognize the need for planning and preparation for recovering people who will be returning to work. Instead, the recovering person often faces this struggle alone.

Recovery at Work deals with fear, shame, false assumptions, unrealistic expectations, sick surroundings, lack of understanding, stigma, impatience, pressures to perform, lack of corporate value for recovery, return to old work patterns, and so on.

Carol Cox Smith is uniquely qualified to give advice on these multifaceted problems. She is a gifted writer, having authored books and numerous magazine articles on career topics. She has had a distinguished career on the roller-coaster of corporate America. She has been through her own personal struggle and has chosen to live a recovering lifestyle. So she writes from personal insight. I think these unique experiences lend a special touch of credibility to her advice. She has accumulated many corporate colleagues and friends, some recovering, some not, who come from all levels of business. She taps many of their stories to flavor the book with reality — at times a brutal reality.

Recovery at Work is full of plans, guidelines, checklists, testimonials, self-tests, do's and don'ts, what if's and what not's.

Many times over I thought, *What a neat way to deal with that problem.* So after I read it over three times, I stole it! This book recognizes that, like everything else we learn in life, facing problems with a simple plan of action gets us on the way to recovery. It does take effort. It does take time and patience. It starts with little steps. It produces little wins. And that is terrific.

There is no question that a lot of people who have personal problems have difficulty seeing their problems. They are blind, and often the company they work for is blind and uncaring about dealing with personal problems such as alcohol and other drug abuse. The company and the bosses don't like the trouble, the lack of productivity, and the accompanying chaos. But as this book points out, a key to solving the massive denial of chemical dependency is *corporate awareness and support.* As with the whole person, the whole corporate value system has to change.

In today's corporate world, there is some movement toward a new core value through workplace wellness and a developed safety net of Employee Assistance Programs. It surely beats hiring and training new staff every time there is a problem. Despite the odds, individuals who face up to their problems and go through some educational or therapeutic experience tend to put forward a newly structured lifestyle. This recovering, chemical-free lifestyle, with a supporting cast of many, is slowly and steadily changing the nature of the workplace.

Recovery at Work is saying, and I agree, that sober, recovering people are likely to be better workers, better risks, and better people for a company than those who have not faced such personal adversity. This may be due to individual insight and the wisdom gained through the confidential discussions of problems in self-help groups.

Individuals who openly discuss their troubled lives in group settings help others make necessary adjustments. Recovering persons, through Alcoholics Anonymous (AA) and Narcotics

Anonymous (NA) or other such groups, have an extended network of emotional and social support anywhere they go, for life. These support groups function as an adjunct to families in providing the feedback that helps people create alternatives to alcohol and other drugs to solve their problems.

Alternatives are embodied in the culture of recovery. And that is what *Recovery at Work* helps explain. The first steps are the Twelve Steps of AA or similar self-help group guidelines that form a blueprint for living this lifestyle. The pitfalls along the way require thought, hard work, contemplation, listening, and a new kind of kindness and gentleness, as contrasted to the all-too-familiar patterns of distrust and chaos of the chemically dependent lifestyle.

Recovery at Work goes the extra yard in quarterbacking a game plan for the recovering person who may be fighting to keep, save, or change his or her job.

In short, *Recovery at Work* is a book for the recovering person, but it is also a book for many others in the recovering person's circle of co-workers and friends. It advocates creative change. It bashes the stigma that a drunk or a junkie is doomed to failure. It raises the expectations of success and suggests many practical steps that can be taken to make better use of opportunities that are available. People who have squarely faced their personal problems and now are ready for the rest of their lives should be encouraged with *Recovery at Work* in hand.

UNIVERSITY OF MINNESOTA
MINNEAPOLIS, MINN.

JAMES M. SCHAEFFER, PH.D.
Director, Alcohol and Other Drug
Abuse Prevention,
School of Public Health

ACKNOWLEDGMENTS

I deeply appreciate the help of all those who shared their history, contributed their expertise, or offered their advice. I am grateful for every book and pamphlet you lent, every film you let me view, every referral you gave me, and every conversation we shared.

Special thanks to Gene Hawes, Jim Kelly, and Ed Nash for helping me get started and sticking with me to the finish.

Thanks to Linda Barbenol, James E. Challenger, Richard V. Croghan, Cornelius "Jim" Finnen, Jerry Fletcher, Ed Furtado, Ilsa Gay, Frank Griffin, Jonathan Hartshorne, Jan Hosea, J. Marlene Hurst, Karen Klett, Frances Lee Menlove, Robert J. Meyers, Dr. Brian Miscall, Dr. George Nash, Josi Hilgers-Noyes, Jaynee Parnegg, Herman Romero, B. L. Ryan, Andrew Sherwood, Susan Silvano, Dr. Gary L. Simpson, Ron Smock, Dr. Bobby Sykes, Wayne Wear, JoAnne Cisneros-West, Olga Wieser, and Nancy Willis.

Heartfelt gratitude to the recovering persons who inspired me with their courage and generosity. Out of respect for their anonymity, I have changed most names and some job descriptions, but all other details are real. All of their quotes are real. All of their recoveries are real. As far as possible, incidents are related with the knowledge and the permission of the person involved.

INTRODUCTION

Whenever I attend a support group meeting, talk to an addictions counselor, visit a treatment center, or share with another recovering friend, the discussion often focuses on career problems. Getting fired, getting hired, starting a new job, walking off an old one, feeling stressed, being passed over for promotion — the ups and downs of the working world create ups and downs in our lives.

We spend many waking hours either working or thinking about work. Often, we spend more time with people from work than with our spouses and children. Work becomes an extension of ourselves, a tangible record of our talents and abilities. It gives us a sense of value, meaning, and purpose.

At the least, career problems and pressures are unsettling. For those who still hold their job, daily pressures can get them down.

- A computer engineer fumes over a confrontation with her boss.
- A business consultant feels frustrated because a proposal flopped.
- A stockbroker needs to make a career change, but worries about his future.

- A real estate agent is irate because another agent stole her client.
- A building contractor rages because the city won't issue vital permits.
- A carpenter is angry because someone stole the tools from his truck.

Such crises may not drive these people back to drink or drugs — but they *can*. Even when people stay clean and sober, such work-related upsets can bring self-doubt, temporary emotional turmoil, and spiritual unrest — pretty miserable stuff.

Whether in recovery or not, few things upset people more than trouble on the job. No matter how smoothly other aspects of your life are running, your job can throw you into a spin. Your emotions — anger, fear, and frustration — can spill over and affect your marriage, your health, your recovery.

People getting help at inpatient or outpatient treatment centers face special kinds of career crises. Often, they feel confused and fearful, dreading returning to work, wondering what will happen when they do. While they may have the support of their boss and company, they worry about "what everyone will think." Recovering people's fears can paralyze them and keep them clinging to the treatment center as a safe haven or to a support group as a hiding place. Counselors and recovering friends try to help them confront their fears and learn coping behaviors, but the transition back to work may still be a terrifying, doubt-filled experience.

Many recovering persons have no job, no career to go back to, even though they are now clean and sober. They can't return to their old career, and they don't have the skills, time, or money to start a new one. They know they need to work, to support themselves. But doing what, where, how? Who will hire them with their tainted work record?

Then there are the nagging questions all recovering persons face:

- If I return to the same workplace, will I go back to old, sick patterns?
- How can I stay clean and sober when all my co-workers drink and use?
- If I practice my recovery program, can I be successful or will I lose my edge?
- Can the business concepts of *excellence* and *high performance* coexist with the recovery concepts of *serenity* and *health?*

Underlying all these problems, doubts, and questions is the fear of failure. When we fail, our self-esteem may plummet, at least temporarily. We may believe we've lost the respect of others. We panic over lack of money, and our inner self tells us, *If you cannot work, you cannot support yourself, and that means you are worthless, nobody, nothing.*

But if we can put in a good day's work with adequate pay, we are more likely to feel worthwhile. This achievement encourages us to believe we can take care of ourselves and remain independent. For the recovering alcoholic or addict, such feelings help build lasting emotional, mental, physical, and spiritual well-being.

At least one study confirms the relationship between career satisfaction and recovery. It states, " ... extensive research and experience have shown that the alcoholic's chances of staying sober are improved if he or she has a satisfying, steady job."[1]*

Such research supports the need for a book that helps recovering persons

- find the right job in the right career field;
- regain and keep their status within their company, industry or profession;
- repair their damaged working relationships;

---

* Editor's note: An Endnotes section, which lists footnotes in each chapter, appears at the end of every chapter in this book.

- understand their career-related feelings;
- face the reality of job discrimination, financial problems, and company restrictions;
- avoid slips;
- and, at the same time, strengthen their personal lives and encourage a strong recovery.

Recovery at Work is one of the first books to tackle the many complex career issues facing recovering alcoholics and addicts. Its message is that a healthy recovery and a satisfying career can go hand in hand.

I bring to this book fourteen years in the corporate world, seven years in the educational field, eight years as a career writer and consultant, and six years of recovery. In addition, I bring to you the experience of dozens of recovering career persons who share their ups and downs. You will also hear from treatment professionals, career counselors, management consultants, executive recruiters, employee assistance directors, addictionologists, psychologists, medical doctors, and corporate leaders.

I hope you will be helped by our collective experience and enjoy success in your recovery at work.

ENDNOTES
Introduction

1. George M. Hunt and N. H. Azrin, "A Community-Reinforcement Approach to Alcoholism," *Behavioral Research and Therapy* 11 (1973): 93.

CHAPTER ONE

A NEW APPROACH
TO YOUR CAREER

Recovery is the beginning, not the end, of your career. That statement may be hard to believe from where you stand now — especially if your present circumstances look anything but promising.

Perhaps you are a treatment center patient, trying to learn new concepts and make major life changes in only four to six weeks. Perhaps you are an unwilling participant in an outpatient treatment program ordered by your boss or a judge. Perhaps you are a confused and frightened newcomer to a Twelve Step support group. Perhaps your career came to a crashing halt when you were forced into a halfway house, hospital, or prison.

You may already have spent months or years of sobriety or drug-free living, but you are still struggling to keep a job, *any* job. You may feel so guilty, so worthless that you cannot bring yourself to answer a classified ad or telephone a potential employer.

You may be picking yourself up and starting all over — from the bottom. You may have destroyed a high-paying career and alienated friends who tried to help you. Now you look around and wonder if anyone will ever take a chance on you again. You know getting back on top will take time and effort — and luck.

You may look around and heave a sigh of relief. You held on to your job. You did not damage your career irreparably — you just dented it here and there. Yet, you may wonder if your boss trusts you, if your co-workers respect you. You worry that you will be denied promotion or passed over for important assignments. You imagine people are talking about you, and not with the kindest intentions.

Wherever you stand now, no matter what your situation, feelings, or imaginings, *recovery is the beginning of your career.*

IMPROVED PERFORMANCE

Recovery at work means learning attitudes and behaviors that lead to success. The roadblocks that kept you from working to your potential start to roll away. You find new energy, new health, new *natural* highs, new satisfactions, sounder relationships, better appearance, smoother disposition, clearer mind, and stronger character. Not all right away and not all simultaneously. But you begin to collect *gains instead of losses.*

These gains make you a valuable employee. Says Jim Kelly of Jim Kelly Counseling Associates and Employee Assistance Director for Sandia National Laboratories:

> If he does something about his problem, then we've got a rehabilitated employee, *a better employee than one that never had the problem.* The person who is totally abstinent from any mood-altering drugs is never going to have a hangover, never have the shakes, never be headachy, never spend money where he shouldn't. He won't be doing things that are unacceptable socially or professionally. He's always going to be *operating at peak efficiency.*

In recovery, then, your performance *improves.* Research and experience show that recovering persons get better jobs and earn more income.[1] One study found that recovering persons earned twice as much as alcoholics or addicts who are still drinking or using.

Why the difference in earning power? People who still drink or use are often unemployed, underemployed, or unmotivated; they do not put out top effort on the job, even though they may think they work to full capacity.

Subtle changes in attitude and work habits affect the performance of the drinking alcoholic or other drug abuser. He or she is often preoccupied with getting and using the drug of choice. He plans an early lunch, comes back late, and leaves work before anyone notices how he slurs his words. She sneaks off to the women's room three or four times more frequently than other employees (to buy or use, or both).

Meanwhile, the employer starts to notice. Absences, tardiness, unexplained disappearances, unreliability, erratic mood swings, accidents, customer or co-worker complaints, financial or family difficulties, and encounters with the law — these flag the addicted person as a problem employee. Problem employees usually do not get promoted and do not earn salary increases.

Alcoholics and other drug abusers seldom see their behavior clearly. They complain that the boss does not appreciate their efforts, their work load is too heavy, or their support staff too light. Their excuses for lowered performance range from "poor economic conditions" to "problems at home." They blame everyone and everything but themselves. As their attitude turns sour, their working relationships spoil. No one wants to work with a person who is surly, argumentative, self-pitying, and uncooperative. As others turn away, the still-suffering alcoholic or other drug abuser becomes less and less effective.

NEW OPPORTUNITIES

On the other hand, the recovering person can operate at peak efficiency. A clear head, renewed health, and improved attitudes open new career doors.

Recovering people can pull themselves out of the confusion and indecision that keeps them trapped in the wrong job, doing the wrong things for the wrong reasons. They can look at themselves and their skills and abilities realistically and find the right way to use their natural talents. They can also establish more honest and open working relationships that lead to better all-around performance and job satisfaction.

These changes work like a magnet to attract new opportunities. Says one recovering woman who owns a successful management consulting firm:

> Up to three years ago, I was simply trying to make as much money as I could. That was how I measured my success. That was the idea that got me sick. Now I use a different ruler. I look for opportunities that fit my goals. It takes scrupulous honesty. If it does fit, I'm inspired and excited.
>
> Many businesses come to me — so many opportunities are out there — the problem is to pursue the right ones. Some of them are so big, they'd overwhelm me and my company. But it's tempting to take them on, anyway. My biggest problem is to have the wisdom and courage to say no when an opportunity comes to me.

Says a recovering man who is an ex-oil company executive:

> When you recover, you can return to society and a productive life. You don't have to be confined and protected from alcohol. Alcohol is no longer the issue. You can hold responsible positions, be on the boards of companies, and the opportunities just open up to you. You become aware of them. A successful career goes hand in hand with a successful recovery. You can grow in a career if you can grow spiritually in your recovery. As that is affirmed and grows within you, then that confidence, the belief in yourself, creates growth.

The stories of opportunities number in the hundreds of thousands. Every person who takes recovery seriously; who recognizes it as a lifesaving, life-enhancing process; who utilizes support and aftercare programs, counseling, friendship, and sponsorship; and who has the perseverance to look inside for discovery and rebirth — every one will become more open to the phenomena of suddenly opened doors, unexpectedly opportune meetings, and plain old-fashioned lucky breaks.

Here are a few of the career turnarounds I heard about while researching this book.

- Pauline rose from a university fine arts instructor to department head, with a significant salary increase. Later, she returned to school to study mental health counseling. After heading up the university's Employee Assistance Program, she resigned to start her own counseling practice.
- Clint went back to his first love, ranching; now, he earns slightly less money, but basks in the freedom of high-mountain country.
- Diane rose from an account executive at a major corporation to president of her own business.
- Ted regained his medical license and reestablished a thriving practice.
- Bruce, who worked for a small plumbing firm, started his own plumbing business. After a slow start, he recently landed a lucrative contract with a large building contractor.
- George, a former insurance salesman, now runs a major insurance conglomerate.
- Edna took a correspondence course in accounting and later became her company's training director.
- Phyllis, a widow without experience or skills, works with the city's biggest and best fashion consultant, doing workshops and private consultations for a growing clientele.

Through your recovery, your new life of health and purpose, you can join other recovering people who have proved themselves successful. They make their own opportunities by taking charge of their life, taking responsibility for the results of their effort or lack of it, and staying healthy in mind, body, and spirit.

Redefining Success

In recovery, success takes on new, deeper meaning. It can be experienced in various ways; but basically, recovering people find success by turning away from outside approval and rewards, and by looking inside for satisfaction, approval, and joy. If the money is good, so much the better, but money never takes first place. The change in how you define success happens *inside,* not outside.

In the past, you may have confused visible signs of success with real success. A private office, a hefty bonus, or the deference of co-workers may have fooled you into feeling successful. But real success means experiencing satisfaction with yourself *as a person,* regardless of outside factors. It means enjoying the *process* of your work, regardless of results. In recovery, success takes on expanded meaning; now you seek satisfaction and wholeness in every area of your life.

As I said in "Success on Your Own Terms," an article I wrote for *The Executive Female* magazine:

> Fulfillment. Satisfaction. Whatever you call it, everyone wants it. But often, there's an empty space between your expectations and reality. As a high-powered male lawyer says, "I'm doing well as a professional, but failing as a person."
>
> Feelings like these are the reason many men and women are making choices that are setting a new standard for success: a well-rounded life. And they're making hard choices to achieve it.
>
> Career success is only one facet of a successful life. Consider your personal growth, health, relationships, community activities, religion and other interests. Defining success on your own terms is essential to wholeness. And wholeness is essential to happiness.[2]

In recovery, you may need to take a new approach to your career if the old way made you sick and miserable. Recovering men and women are more likely to find success and satisfaction in understanding, growth, and balance than in power, money, or prestige (although those make nifty side benefits).

For some, this new concept of success brings a deep sense of relief. It lifts the burden to prove yourself to others, to live by others' standards, to struggle to cross the chasm between where you are and where you want to be.

Here is what Red, a recovering alcoholic and car salesman, says about his success in recovery. Although his work pace has slowed, his results have improved.

> My values are changing. Material things are not as important as enjoying my life. There's a need to produce, but not to impress people or be Number One — that obsession to achieve, to be tops. I was a workaholic. I started work at five in the morning and didn't quit until eleven at night. Now I'm doing a better job without the obsession. I'm not thinking about drinking or getting a fix. I'm more relaxed, less stressed. Things work out without forcing, without struggling. My customers knew I had a problem. Now I spend more quality time with them, and they see the difference.

Like Red, you may have defined success as

> . . . having it all: all the money, admiration, power, and respect I can handle. Owning lots of *stuff*. Doing lots of *things*. Knowing I'm the best and that other people know it too.

But now, in recovery, that definition no longer works. Your new definition might go something like this:

> Success is staying sober and drug free. It means feeling good about myself. Knowing I'm doing the right thing. Taking responsibility for myself and my actions. Helping others. Making the choices that are best for me. Making a commitment to recovery. Living with honor.

11

You will discover that this definition works for millions of recovering men and women. Perhaps your financial situation never improves. Perhaps your home and car always need repair and your clothes look noticeably dated. Perhaps *stuff* and *things* never come your way. But you will still be a success, because you are living a clean and sober life.

In recovery, then, success includes three qualities: (1) expanded opportunities, (2) changed values, and (3) inner satisfaction. The following stories are about two recovering people whose success in both career and life show what can be done when recovery is taken seriously.

He Went to Skid Row and Back

Here is a man who had it all — and threw it away like an empty pint bottle. He sat on the board of directors of an oil field specialty service company. He took home a six-figure income, but blew it on alimony, wrecked cars, and three-week binges. He rose so high in the company, he thought no one could touch him — until the president gave him a warning he did not heed.

In the 1950s, Alan was an overnight success, a "boy wonder." After he joined a Houston oil company, he quickly climbed from sales manager to vice president of marketing. With his affinity for hard work and his outward air of confidence, he was selected as general manager of the company's new subsidiary, a plum position that put him on the parent company's board.

He had the outward appearance of success. Yet, inside, his confidence crumbled. He needed to drink to cope. Instead of the confident decision-maker that his job demanded, Alan became a hesitant, indecisive procrastinator.

Eventually, management noticed. The president talked to Alan confidentially about his disappearances, his startling changes in personality. Alan was becoming hard to get along with, always blaming something or somebody. He was especially irritable and edgy before and during board meetings (Alan stayed away from alcohol for two days before a meeting so he would not shake or throw up).

Alan put himself into an inpatient treatment program with the president's approval. The president, however, added this threat: "One slip and you're out." Fifty-eight days after leaving the hospital, Alan drank again. He was out.

But Alan had a back-up plan, an offer with a national company that was entering the oil field business. They needed his experience and contacts; he needed a refuge. For the first three months, Alan stayed sober. But he started to drink again, and his drinking rapidly progressed. Eleven months later, he found himself on Skid Row.

He failed another try at sobriety in a state hospital and yet another in a Skid Row detoxification center. Then he took a "geographical cure" and moved to Denver. He was drunk when he got off the plane. Summoning all his remaining strength, he detoxed himself in a motel room and walked across the street to a meeting of Alcoholics Anonymous.

Amazingly, once he sobered up, he had little trouble finding another job. As his sobriety progressed, so did his career. Through industry contacts, he started his own oil drilling rig business. Then came the drop in the price of oil, and he lost millions. But he held on to his sobriety.

As Alan approached his ten-year AA birthday, he was bankrupt and burned out on the oil industry. He turned to his second love: helping recovering alcoholics. He served on the board of a detox facility for indigents and tried to organize an Employee Assistance Program for small businesses. Although this new business plan never materialized, he gained valuable contacts in the recovery field. Through these friends, he became a treatment facility marketing representative. He works in that position today, earning less than one-tenth of the money his oil rig business netted him. He sees his new career as an opportunity to offer recovery to others, the same opportunity that was given to him. Alan feels happy with himself and excited about his future.

"I get excited about what I'm doing here. And one opportunity leads to another. When I was drinking, nothing happened. I couldn't allow it to. What's so beautiful is the awareness that so much is available to me. So many opportunities.

"The further I get into sobriety, the more I realize the tremendous impact my drinking had on my career. I can beat myself to death, looking back. Having to live in a one-bedroom apartment, compared to where I came from. Then I realize I'm right where I need to be.

"What we have to look at is our values. I've had to work through some financial hardships, making the adjustments. But my values have changed. They're more honest and more pure than they used to be. I've changed from loving money and success to loving God. I have everything I need, and I'm happy, even though I don't have financial freedom. That's okay.

"In my case, even though I went into bankruptcy and lost my business, there was a purpose in what happened. I was forced to make changes. It deepened my faith; it changed into trust that everything will be okay."

Everything will be more than okay. With a solid core of business strength, reinforced by sobriety and faith, Alan sees opportunities in every direction.

Full of energy and enthusiasm, this former millionaire, this former Skid Row derelict, faces life with the inner strength of someone who knows himself, knows his assets, and knows his business. Whatever that business turns out to be, Alan will succeed.

She Said "Yes" to Recovery

Five years ago, Diane suffered from alcoholism and compulsive overwork. Her career was the center of her life, consuming all her energy. She tried to prove herself over and over again, struggling for years to make up for her alcoholic father's dismal failures, longing to win approval from her rival sister and recognition from her status-oriented mother. She pushed herself to compete aggressively and lose what she considered "feminine weaknesses." She wanted to be looked at, not as a female, but as a capable executive.

She became bored with marriage and family life, and preferred the excitement of drinking and drugging. Her hard-working, hard-playing lifestyle led to separation and annulment. Although her marriage crashed, her career skyrocketed. She climbed higher and higher up the corporate organizational chart, gaining more prestige with each promotion. But her ambition poured pressure and stress on every interaction or transaction that involved her career. She was tormented by perfectionism and by thoughts of failure.

Amazingly, her drinking did little damage to her corporate status, but it destroyed her self-esteem. She suffered from self-doubt and from the consuming fear that she would never reach her goals. Her fear was flamed by the confusion and demoralization that come with active alcoholism.

When she finally sought help, she was totally out of balance, her mental and emotional health shattered. In desperation, she called AA and a woman came to talk to her. "God sent me the right person. Outside, she was the exact opposite of me. But inside, she was everything I wanted to be." She clung to this first sponsor and a women's support group for strength, courage, and en-

15

couragement. As the years progressed, she began to regain her balance and to see her career as only one part of a full and satisfying life.

Recently, Diane was offered the presidency of a national corporation — her lifelong goal was within reach. Calmly, without a regret, she turned it down. The old Diane would have jumped at the chance; her ego would have taken over and compelled her to accept. But the new Diane knew better. She had found a new way of living and she refused to sacrifice it for gold letters on her office door.

"The reason I turned it down was my recovery. What seemed important at one time doesn't seem important any longer. I had worked so hard and long for this one moment in my life, but I did not hesitate to turn it down. When that moment came, my priorities were different and I was balanced. That was a tremendous step for me to take, and because I took it, I came out a better person."

Instinctively, Diane knew something bigger was waiting for her. She stayed another year with the firm, and then she saw an opportunity to go into her own business.

Now the president of her own company, Diane enjoys her dual roles of dynamic businessperson and recovering human being. Her recovery program helps her balance her career and personal life as she strives to grow spiritually. Success is no longer the whip that drives her toward illness and despair; it is the *reward of wellness.*

Diane's career has all three qualities of a successful recovery: expanded opportunities, changed values, and inner satisfaction. Like Alan, she learned to put her recovery *first.* As a result, without pushing or shoving, manipulating or lying, abusing themselves or punishing others, they found a success they can *live* with.

TAKING A NEW APPROACH

As you analyze the success stories in this chapter and throughout the book, you will discover that recovering people approach their job in ways that seem strange, sometimes bizarre, to the ordinary man or woman. Yet, the experience of thousands of recovering people has shown that a different approach is essential to a healthy recovery. The old way put you on the fast track to pressure, stress, frustration, resentment — and illness. On the recovery road, we develop new priorities that lead to both a successful recovery and a successful career. Here are some ways that have worked for others. Think about them. Try one, then two, then all. You will begin to feel comfortable with them and to integrate them into your life. When you do, like Alan and Diane, your career will take on a new dimension.

Put Your Recovery First

Many of us feel uneasy with the idea of putting our recovery first. As businesspeople, we may have put our career first and have overvalued achievement, results, and rewards. We worked late, took work home, ate cold dinners at the office, missed family get-togethers, and cancelled vacation plans.

Sometimes that approach worked; we *did* achieve success. More often, we encountered failure and frustration. These two terrors can drive a person to find relief in addictive substances or compulsions, or they can *excuse* a person's destructive behavior.

Putting our recovery first means making decisions and taking action based on what best promotes our mental, emotional, physical, and spiritual health. Career advancement takes second place. This new approach requires effort, especially because it feels strange to us. But we must try a healthier approach to handling business situations, from small annoyances to monumental crises.

This change can mean taking a further, even more difficult step: believing that, if we put our recovery first, our business

17

problems will resolve themselves to our best interest. We do what is best for us, and trust that the result will turn out well. Giving up drinking alcohol, using other drugs, or any compulsive behavior may look *easy* compared to giving up an attitude we have lived with all our adult life.

For example, Sharon, a senior accountant for a major credit card company, tried it and came out on top of a combustible situation.

> At thirty-two, Sharon has the outward appearance of a no-nonsense career woman. But inside, she is sensitive, insecure, and frightened. She is one year into recovery; her emotions still run high, and she sometimes overreacts when she feels threatened.
>
> Sharon was startled a few weeks ago when the financial vice president announced that Internal Revenue Service auditors would be checking Sharon's department within two days. She knew her accounts were in order, so she did not worry. Then, one hour before the auditors' arrival, the vice president dropped a stack of files on Sharon's desk and told her they were her responsibility; she had to get them straightened out — and she had one hour to do it! Sharon stared at the stack and felt fear and anger rush through her whole body.
>
> Sharon had three choices. She could stick with her old approach and get into a no-win argument with the vice president; she could frantically try to complete the work in the next hour; or she could get out of a situation that was potentially dangerous to her recovery, regroup, and tackle the problem when she felt calmer. She chose to get out. She said not a single word, rose abruptly, and left the office. When she fled, she headed straight to a support group meeting where she vented her anger, listened to comments, regained her composure, and gathered courage to return to the threatening situation.

When she returned to the office, the stack of files still lay on her desk, and the IRS auditors had arrived. She sat at her desk calmly, working at her usual steady pace, waiting for them to talk to her. When they finally did, she told them simply and honestly, without hysteria, what had happened and showed them her other files, all in order. She says:

"The head man commended me for my honesty. He could clearly see what had happened — it was pretty obvious. He told me that he could see from my other files that I was caught up on my work and that I had done a good job. He told me to take time and get everything done the way it was supposed to be, and he would come back later and check it out."

Putting her recovery first gave Sharon an immediate advantage. It prevented her from overreacting and intensifying an explosive encounter. It helped her feel in control of her life, not a victim of another person's inefficiency. Eventually, her smooth demeanor and nonblaming honesty won her management recognition.

Plan Your Day Around Recovery Activities

You probably keep an appointment calendar on your desk at home or at work. Perhaps you put a daily reminder pad in your purse or wallet and cross-check your appointments when you get back to your desk. Whatever method you use to remember dates and places, make your recovery activities your first entry.

Too often, business obligations get us going at a frantic pace. No time for lunch, for conversation, for a deep breath. We promise ourselves *today* we will exercise or eat three solid meals or read an inspirational book or call a recovering friend. Then we check our calendar and see we have left no time for those healthy activities. By the end of the day, we are exhausted, drained, so tired we cannot drag ourselves to a support group meeting. Another day passes without doing something to promote our well-being.

Instead, schedule what you will do today to aid your recovery, such as reading recovery literature, attending a support group or aftercare meeting, meditating, or helping another person. Make these commitments *first*, then schedule other appointments around them.

Avoid Confrontations Or
Learn to Handle Them Constructively

What kind of on-the-job situations upset you? What causes you to feel instantly angry, fearful, guilty, apologetic, worried, bewildered, or defeated? When you recognize the feeling or reaction, you must quickly identify your options and act on the best one for your recovery.

If finding spelling errors in your correspondence makes your stomach ache, you have several options. Find a firm, but kind, way to talk to your secretary about improving his or her spelling; buy a dictionary and show him or her how to use it; ask another secretary to proofread your letters; get another secretary who can spell; or just sign your name and ignore the errors. What option you choose does not matter; any one will work. What does matter is choosing the option that makes you feel good and returns you to a peaceful state.

If you hate being kept waiting and you must meet with a client who is always thirty minutes behind schedule, cancel the meeting; get him or her to come to your office so you can continue working; go to his or her office and arrive thirty minutes late yourself; or take along some recovery literature to read while you wait. Says Melody Beattie in *Codependent No More:*

> Learn to recognize when you're reacting, when you are allowing someone or something to yank your strings. . . . Figure out what you need to do to take care of yourself. Make your decisions based on reality, and

make them from a peaceful state. If you can't get peaceful about a decision, let it go. It's not time to make it yet Wait until your mind is consistent and your emotions are calm.[3]

Stay in the Present

Career men and women are accustomed to looking ahead, making plans, projecting sales, setting goals. We want to take care of all future contingencies.

The problem is that we end up worrying about and trying to control events that have not happened — and may never happen. We make decisions based on imagined worst possibilities. We never imagine we will ask for a raise and get it without a fuss. We never imagine we will easily qualify as the best person to head up that new branch office.

Stay in the present. Concentrate fully on what you are doing right now. You need to prepare adequately to meet your responsibilities, but you need not dwell on them. By staying in the present, you can enjoy each task more and complete it more efficiently.

Sometimes, when my thoughts are scattered, I focus all my senses on whatever I am doing at that moment. For example, if I am showering, I concentrate fully on the sting of the spray against my face, the fragrance of the soap, the warmth of a terry towel. I experience it fully, and I calm my feelings of being scattered and uneasy. This technique can help you feel calmer and more controlled, and your work will net better results.

Establish New Work Patterns

We need to change harmful work habits to healthier ones, but such changes take time. Most of us try to change everything at once, and we become discouraged when our efforts to revolutionize our lives flop miserably. Instead, make one small change, become accustomed to it, praise yourself for your accomplishment, and go on to the next change.

For example, if you want to get to work on time, you may need to get up earlier. Go slowly — your body will rebel if you shake it awake an hour or two before your usual wake-up time. Go to bed fifteen minutes earlier and set your alarm fifteen minutes earlier. Practice this schedule for a week, then try moving your bedtime and alarm clock another fifteen minutes. Eventually, you will adjust your whole cycle.

Be patient with yourself if you revert to old patterns. They are deeply entrenched and not about to give up without a fight. Says behavioral consultant Bobby Sykes, Employee Assistance Director for Digital Equipment Corporation:

> Develop a reasonable success ratio. Success is a strong motivator for continued work. If you adopt too big a goal at once, chances for success are reduced. If you fail repeatedly, there is a punishment aspect that reduces your drive to make changes. Engage in very small changes until you become stronger. As you strengthen, you begin to bite off larger challenges.

You may need to make changes in the way you relate to others on the job.

> Before recovery, Andrew, a computer engineer, wanted everyone at work to like him. Shy and uncommunicative, he sought the approval of co-workers by asking for extra work. At lunch time, while others left the office, Andrew worked straight through, never stopping to eat or relax. He used that time to help other engineers complete projects. Everyone liked him, accepted him, and used him.
>
> In recovery, Andrew needed to make changes. For one, he needed to start an exercise program and build up his body with three square meals a day. Although he was

afraid his co-workers would no longer like him, he decided to make a healthy change. Instead of working during his lunch hour, he left the office and either ate a bag lunch under a shady tree or joined his wife at a nearby cafeteria.

Did his co-workers reject him? "They were a little puzzled at first," says Andrew, "but I explained what I was doing and they accepted it. I thought not doing extra work would affect my job rating. But I wasn't even supposed to be doing the extra work, so when I stopped, it didn't affect my position at all."

Change should take place gradually. To keep yourself going in the right direction, surround yourself with things that remind you of your new behavior: books, magazines, posters, T-shirts — anything that inspires you. Associate with others who encourage and support you. *Ask* for their support and suggestions. Avoid persons who criticize you or the changes you're making. Old friends, for example, may not want you to change and may insist they liked you better the way you were.

At the end of each day, look back and evaluate how well you followed your course of change. Identify obstacles and figure out what you will do tomorrow to stay on target. You may find that keeping a diary or journal helps you pinpoint recurring problems. Talk to yourself and give yourself encouragement. Then, do what many people feel very uncomfortable doing: talk to someone else.

Talk Over Problems

You cannot get well, you cannot rebuild your life, you cannot find real success *alone.* It did not work before, and it will not work now. According to Terence Gorski and Merlene Miller in *Staying Sober:*

> You cannot recover in isolation. Total recovery involves the help and support of a variety of persons. You need others for a successful relapse prevention plan. . . .

You must be willing to talk with these people on a regular basis so they will notice when something is going wrong. You must also be willing to listen and act upon what they say.[4]

Fortunately, plenty of people are ready to give you a hand. You can find the help you need from a support group, sponsor, supportive boss, employee assistance person, counselor, recovering friend, or spiritual advisor. If family members are in recovery, they may be helpful, if you respect their needs in return. Gorski and Miller say, "Remember, too, that the members of your family are also recovering. You must acknowledge their needs and make a strong commitment to assist them in their own recovery programs."[5]

If family members are not in recovery, they may be too involved in their own misery to be of help. As you progress in recovery, they will likely gain confidence in you and renew their trust. But right now, no matter how much they care about you, they may not be able to listen to your problems and tell you what you need to hear to steady yourself.

For recovery-based help, you need persons who are knowledgeable about recovery principles or who are practicing a recovery program. These persons help, not by giving advice, but by listening to you and helping you find your own solutions.

Karen, a sportswear buyer who travels frequently, tucks her telephone list of Narcotics Anonymous friends inside her handbag whenever she leaves town. As soon as Karen settles into her hotel room, she telephones the local NA office and gets a list of meetings. She attends at least one meeting, even if she must reschedule a business appointment. She takes time after the meeting to talk to other NA members about her trip and any difficulties she is having. She gets more telephone numbers from local members and calls two or three friends before she leaves. Wherever Karen goes, she takes her recovery friends with her — at least in spirit.

After four years in recovery, Karen no longer feels embarrassed to telephone friends and discuss a problem. She knows that reaching out helps both her and the other person. Even a quick five-minute talk can bolster both persons' courage and self-esteem for the rest of the day.

Some newcomers to recovery (and even some old-timers) feel awkward about picking up the telephone or going out for coffee to talk things over. Once you realize that this is exactly what you are supposed to do, these guidelines may help you get started and make sharing more comfortable:

1. Ask if this is a convenient time to talk. If not, set a time to call back.

Business responsibilities take precedence over your needs, at least during working hours. But, your call may provide a welcome distraction, a few minutes of friendship and sanity in a frantic day.

2. Tell how much time you need and briefly describe the general situation.

Say, "I need about ten minutes to talk about my presentation this afternoon. I'm feeling fearful, and I'd really like your suggestions." This briefing helps the other person evaluate your needs, get the appropriate attitude, and set a mental clock. Stick to your time limit. When your time ends, thank the person and sign off. Do not try to eke out another five minutes, unless your friend offers.

3. Report the outcome.

You have asked someone's help and now he or she deserves to know the results. Later, after your problem or situation is resolved, tell your friend what happened. Offer your thanks again.

Perhaps you think another telephone call or meeting would bother that person unnecessarily. Actually, letting him or her know what happened is a courtesy most people appreciate. It is a subtle form of flattery; it allows the person to feel good about the advice he or she gave, and it gives a deserved pat on the back. It lets both of you feel good about each other. This simple act can reinforce your gratitude and the other person's program.

4. Realize that, if you ask for help about the same problem over and over again, you probably are not listening.

Yes, of course you will encounter situations that repeatedly upset you. But at some point you must take charge of them yourself — do what you are advised to do, make a decision, or accept what is. Instead of looking for more advice, admit that no one can help you but yourself. Then make the best move or decision you can at the moment, and get on with it.

❀ ❀ ❀ ❀ ❀

Recovery is the beginning, not the end, of your career. This statement may alarm you. From where you sit, it may appear impossible, outlandish, and even silly. Yet this idea has proven practical, workable, and achievable for many recovering people over the years. As they continued their recovery program, they encountered dozens of opportunities they previously couldn't imagine. They slowly, perhaps reluctantly, started to change their values. These new values began to eliminate destructive patterns that kept them from realizing their potential, from performing at their peak. They discovered inner strength and self-worth deep inside themselves. You will discover your own power. With these new tools, you can begin to build a personally satisfying career.

In recovery we find open doors and new beginnings, rather than shattered dreams and last chances. Sometimes we stumble over the same mistake again and again, but we can eventually learn to sidestep it or try another route. In time, we may look back and breathe a sigh of relief, knowing that we do not have to take that path again.

ENDNOTES
Chapter One

1. George M. Hunt and N. H. Azrin, "A Community-Reinforcement Approach to Alcoholism," *Behavioral Research & Therapy* 11, (1973):100.

2. Carol Cox Smith, "Success on Your Own Terms," *The Executive Female* 10, No. 5 (September/October 1987): 35.

3. Melody Beattie, *Codependent No More* (Center City, Minn.: Hazelden Educational Materials, 1987), 66-67.

4. Terence T. Gorski and Merlene Miller, *Staying Sober* (Independence, Mo.: Independence Press, 1986), 167-168.

5. Ibid., 169.

CHAPTER TWO

MAKING A SMOOTH TRANSITION

Give yourself credit. You have survived one of the most frightening experiences any human being can face. You confronted your addiction.

You have faced the devastation it caused you and your family. And now you may be seeing its impact on your work life. As you remember missed appointments, lost sales, botched projects, ruined relationships, wasted time, and squandered income, you may feel crushed by a sense of failure.

Yet, this apparent career disaster can be viewed in a more positive way: Today, you are sober and drug-free, and you are starting over with new self-knowledge and new tools for success. With this positive outlook, you can reinterpret past failures and face the future with hope, understanding, and enthusiasm.[1]

THE REENTRY PERIOD

You may be spending four to eight weeks in a treatment center or several months in an outpatient program. You may be gathering strength in a halfway house, hospital ward, or detoxification facility. You may have recently walked into a support group meeting room, joined an aftercare group, or begun therapy or counseling. Wherever you are, you probably hope to get back to work as quickly and painlessly as possible. But the transition may be slower and more difficult than you expect. Belonging to AA, NA, or another support group can help smooth the way.

After starting your recovery, you go through a period that counseling professionals call *reentry*. You take what you have learned back into the workplace, and, wherever possible, integrate recovery principles into your work life. This period may be rough, emotionally, mentally, physically, and financially. But the more time you give it, and the more you learn about yourself and the recovery process, the better chance you have for success. This success depends, in part, on where you are coming from (treatment center, halfway house, outpatient program) and where you are going (supportive workplace, your own business, unemployment line).

Many addiction counselors and Employee Assistance Programs favor outpatient treatment. As an outpatient, you can learn the Twelve Step program through the treatment facility, then practice it daily in the workplace. If you encounter problems, you can discuss them with your counselor and your group. They keep you focused on your recovery and give you support as you work through real-life confrontations.

One of the most difficult transitions happens between a halfway house and a new or probationary job. The National Institute on Alcohol Abuse and Alcoholism (NIAAA) says a halfway house " . . . provides preventive and aftercare services for persons who do not need to be institutionalized but would benefit from a supportive living arrangement."[2] A halfway house gives a resident the opportunity to learn and practice new attitudes and behaviors within a group setting. It can also provide stability to those who have no support network of family or friends, and bring caring people back into their lives. While a halfway house does many good things, it makes only one-half of a transition. The other half, the workplace, must be supportive and nonthreatening. If the other side is a new or probationary job, the transition can be stressful and contribute to relapse.

Perhaps the most difficult route goes from a detoxification ward or prison to the unemployment line. The recovering person gets little or no support from either side. Without any help in between to deal with emotional and financial problems and to learn new job-finding skills, the recovering person is more susceptible to relapse. Being unemployed increases anxiety, depression, fatigue, and confusion and decreases reaction time, dexterity, and problem-solving ability.[3]

In general, then, if you do have a job, you should hold onto it as best you can, unless it seriously threatens your recovery. The old AA adage, "Don't make any major decisions or changes for the first twelve months," makes sense.

A better route takes you from a quality treatment center to a supportive workplace with an effective Employee Assistance Program (EAP). An EAP is an employer- or labor-sponsored service to assist employees, and often their dependents, find help for drug, mental and emotional, family, health, or other personal problems. This route provides inpatient treatment and education, with valuable separation time from job conflicts and pressures, plus a contact person (EAP counselor) within the receiving company. If middle and upper management support and use the EAP program, they help establish a setting into which recovering persons can reintegrate smoothly.

No one transitional route guarantees successful recovery or spells certain failure. Wherever you begin your recovery, wherever you go back to work, you face similar experiences. You come face-to-face with yourself and with your feelings.

DEALING WITH FEELINGS

Most persons in early recovery don't recognize their emotions and cannot handle them even when they do. Their emotions pop up unexpectedly and throw them off balance. Either they don't like their feelings, or they don't feel anything when they know they should. These emotional reactions are normal, especially in early recovery. If you know what to expect, you can accept your emotions and rehearse handling emotional outbursts.

Shock and Mood Swings

Sometimes addicted people turn belligerent when an employer forces them into a treatment center. Sometimes they know they should feel something, anything, but they don't because their emotions go numb.

After shock comes mood swings. Once you feel the full impact of your situation, your feelings will start emerging. You may react with stony silence, preferring isolation over conversation. Or you may want to tell your story to every available ear. You may find yourself crying uncontrollably or angrily throwing things. Your moods may swing wildly from depression to elation, from resentment to gratitude, from quiet to agitation. Disarming as they are, these sudden mood swings are often part of the recovery process, and they will eventually level off.

Four things help overcome shock and stabilize moods.

- The first is education. Learning that you have a *disease*[4] breaks through the numbness and lets you look at your past actions without feeling overwhelming self-blame. Learning how to protect yourself from relapse also takes away much of the underlying fear.
- The second source of help is a plan of action, such as found in a Twelve Step recovery program. The Steps provide focus, direction, a place to start, and a way to proceed in an orderly manner.
- The third helpful shock-reducer is time. You need time to absorb and sort through what has happened — and to heal.
- The fourth is group support. In the safety of group meetings, you can talk about your feelings and ventilate excess emotion. Just as important, you listen to others and develop healthier, more productive ways to express your emotions.

As you return to work, you may continue to float in a state of shock. Mood swings may continue for many months, but don't be alarmed and don't push yourself. Although you will need to make some decisions, this is not the time for major changes. You shouldn't try to reorganize your business, start an important new project, hire or fire an employee, or quit your job, at least for now. Because your reasoning and decision-making powers are diminished, the best course of action is no action at all. When the fog lifts, you can sort things out and make appropriate moves.

Fear and Loneliness

Fear is an integral part of the addictive lifestyle. Active chemically dependent people fear being discovered, losing their drug supply or supplier, not having enough money to buy what they need, not remembering what they did or where they were last night — and they especially fear losing their job. To addicted people, holding their job means holding on to control. It means protecting their source of supply. With regular income, you can buy what you need when you need it.

Using drugs temporarily relieves fear. The substance turns fear to arrogance ("This company is lucky to have me. Look at all I've done for them") or blame ("If these people would run this place right, I wouldn't be in this mess"). As addiction progresses, fear becomes so pervasive it seems normal. Fred, a personnel manager for a public utility firm, said:

> I knew the jig was up. I was actually relieved when my boss talked to me. He told me to get help or get out. It had been coming for a long time, but I wasn't willing to admit it. As soon as I left his office, I called a friend in AA, and he took me to a meeting that night. I didn't know how much fear I had until it was gone.

In early recovery, fear can return and hit you from several directions. While you generally feel good about yourself and the changes you are making, you can also feel uneasy and apprehensive. You may wonder if you can cope with life, with work, and with relationships. Before recovery, drinking or using answered every unpleasant disagreement, every sudden emergency, and every unrelieved pressure. Unfortunately, alcohol and other drugs left you long on addiction and short on coping skills. This is how Robert J. Meyers, Assistant Director for Alcohol/Drug Treatment Programs for University of New Mexico/Bernallilo County Mental Health Center, explained the dilemma:

Healthy, functioning persons have lots of ways to cope. Their ego-defense mechanisms are varied. Alcoholics have one ego-defense mechanism: they drink. They drink when they're angry, sad, fearful, destitute, hopeless, morose. No matter what the problem, they drink. Healthy, functioning people talk to a friend, jog, play tennis, scream into a pillow, go to a therapist, tap dance, go swimming, whatever is comfortable for them. At the same time, they are dealing with the problem in their own way.

Many recovering people are loners. Often, healthier friends and co-workers pulled away as your addiction took control. Friendships with those who use drugs dissolved when you decided to stay clean and sober. Social isolation can be a painful — but temporary — part of your transition to a healthy new lifestyle.

You must develop a whole new set of coping strategies to deal with day-to-day issues. You learn many new strategies in treatment, aftercare, and support group meetings. But you must test each one, not knowing whether it will work or fail. You may feel frightened, unsure of whether you can handle pressures without turning back to your addiction.

Fear fades when you reach out to others for help and realize you are not alone. One source of help is your company Employee Assistance Program counselor. Let him or her refer you to the best resources for physical, psychological, and financial assistance.

A good aftercare counselor, therapist, or sponsor can become your sounding board, someone to give you the feedback to help you understand your fears and take constructive action. You can discuss your feelings, problems, and on-the-job relationships. The more you talk, the less your fears will control you.

Friends help dispel fear. A network of friends can help you evaluate and change your lifestyle.[5] If you are a loner, reaching out to others for friendship takes humility. Your pride tells you, *I can handle it myself,* but your new wisdom tells you, *Talk to someone.* To whom should you talk? *Not* to former friends if the friendships were based on shared addictions. Without addiction, there may be no basis for friendship. In fact, your recovery may seem a threat to, or an indictment of, your friends' lifestyle. As soon as they know you are serious about staying clean and sober, they may openly avoid you. If you go back to the same old haunts and try to maintain the same old friendships, you will feel uncomfortably out of place, and you might start drinking or using again in order to fit in.

In some ethnic and social groups, where a local bar or apartment is the neighborhood hangout, recovering people may feel there are few other places to socialize. When you stay away, you automatically lose contact with your friends. This loss brings anger, loneliness, and despair — dangerous feelings for a recovering person.

To replace those feelings with happier, healthier ones, you need new friends who share your values and appreciate your goals and who can support you. You need new friends who

- don't take drugs;
- are easily available by telephone or personal contact;
- engage in productive conversations and activities;
- keep an encouraging, positive attitude;
- share experiences honestly and openly;

- know and respect your history;
- believe in their own and your spirituality.

You can find such friends, first, in a support group where you are likely to experience easy acceptance and a warm sense of belonging. Second, at work. Persons in a similar business can talk the same language. Third, among persons who enjoy interests similar to yours, such as skiing, body building, or classical music. Your church or school offers ways to make friends if you will only look for them.

Your best friend is the Higher Power who loves and guides you. You may have "fired" your Higher Power years ago, but now that powerful Presence can be a great barrier against fear. Prayer and meditation help you get back in touch with your Higher Power. Just saying "Please" in the morning and "Thank You" at night reopens the conversation. Taking a one-minute prayer break can quickly reduce fear and increase confidence. As one staff member at Los Alamos National Laboratory says:

> I collect sayings and slogans on my bulletin board. I've got prayers, meditations, jokes, cartoons — anything that reminds me of who I am and where I came from. When things get crazy, I have to back off, stop, read, and compose myself, and then I'm okay. Dealing with engineers here is tough. They like to push their weight around. Before, I'd tell them off. Today, I put them on hold and kick back a minute. It's so easy to get into a fight, but I back off. My meditations help me every day.

Some support groups teach the acronym, F.E.A.R. The letters represent "Future Events Appearing Real." You may not know what the future will bring, but you imagine the worst. Instead of projecting, stay in the present. Remind yourself that you are doing fine and that you and your Higher Power will handle any problems that come up, *when* they come up.

Shame

When our behavior draws the disapproving attention of others, we judge ourselves as harshly as they do. We may have grown up afraid of "what people think" and carry that burden into our adult life. Some people see the alcoholic or drug addict as a "bad person, weak and immoral." Fortunately, as one chemical dependency counselor said, this attitude is becoming "un-American." It is also becoming unbusinesslike. Over 75 percent of all Fortune 500 companies have set up some form of an Employee Assistance Program.[6] Recovering people are becoming the new role models of the American business scene. As Worklife Counseling President Jonathan Hartshorne expressed it:

> There is nothing about alcoholism or drug abuse treatment that needs to be hidden. It is a value in our society that people seek this. People who bite the bullet and go to treatment bring truth and courage to the workplace. It's no secret that we're an addictive society. We don't have to hide and be ashamed.

Or, as one recovering alcoholic said proudly:

> Hell! They knew I was a drunk. Why shouldn't they know I'm a *recovering* drunk?

Even while a person recovers, shame may be unexpectedly persistent. One recovering woman, a senior administrative officer with a large health maintenance organization, still suffers shame after one year of sobriety. The daughter of deeply religious parents, she struggles under the weight of her parents' condemnation and the imagined wrath of a punishing God. Because she cannot accept her disease, she accepts the blame and the shame.

Education helps overcome shame. You learn the truth behind the saying, "You're not a bad person trying to get good; you're a sick person trying to get well." You see the addiction as the malevolent entity, not yourself. The addiction is one thing; *you* are another.

Although you may understand and accept your disease, you may still suffer shame, the shame imposed by a less-than-sympathetic world. Many recovering persons fear that exposure will bring loss of job, status, or income. Fear makes them want to stay hidden. As long as no one knows, they believe they are safe. So they tell no one. Their disease becomes a secret shame.

Guilt

Guilt comes from doing something you believe is wrong, or *not doing* something you believe is right. You may have stolen money from your company, pilfered merchandise or equipment to buy alcohol or other drugs, damaged company property, lied, cheated, argued, malingered, abused co-workers, or over-stepped privileges. In recovery, you see your behavior more clearly, and you recognize its impact on yourself and others. Now you feel guilty for what you have done.

But feeling guilty doesn't get you anywhere. You can crank up guilt and self-pity all you want to, but your recovery won't get moving until you make a commitment to remedy the past and develop strategies to avoid those behaviors. In Twelve Step programs, Step Eight, Step Nine, and Step Ten provide a plan of action to do exactly that. These steps suggest that you make a list of all persons you have harmed and make direct amends to each one; then take daily inventories of your behavior; and when you are wrong, admit it. Guilt resolved in this manner can strengthen your recovery because you are no longer making excuses. You are facing your past and taking responsibility for your mistakes.

You may feel guilt unnecessarily because you believe you are not living up to your or others' expectations. You "should" be doing something you are not (like working harder, staying later, taking on extra assignments). You may feel guilt because you resent the people trying to help you: your boss, your counselor, your co-workers, your support group, or your family. When you are unable to vent your resentment or resolve it, you can turn it against yourself. The result brings the sickening emotion of self-pity. As Don, a safety and security officer, says:

> My biggest problem was getting rid of resentments. It's the most useless, wasteful of all emotions. I resented people imposing their will on my life. I thought I was doing fine up until they started telling me what to do. In treatment, I was diagnosed as very depressed — "wallowing in self-pity," they said. It was even worse when I got out of treatment and went back to work.

Guilt for *your* behavior that is directed at others (resentment) can drive you back to your addiction. It should be treated with large doses of self-awareness, self-acceptance, admission of your part in causing your problems, and an honest look at the motives that underlie your emotions. If shame creeps in, share your feelings with others who appreciate you. Don's resentments and self-pity are gradually dissipating as he learns to accept himself as he is — and others as they are. He allows himself to talk to a few people at work about his recovery. As he progresses, his work performance improves and his resentments decrease. He says, "I get satisfaction from doing something well. It acts like a medicine."

Anger

When you were drinking and using, anger kept people away from you. Now, in recovery, anger can be a lethal weapon. It can keep you constantly upset, never knowing when it will explode. Others are wary of you, wondering when your next outburst will blast them. Where does anger come from?

You may blame others for your past mistakes and present unhappiness, and take your anger out on them, or you may blame yourself and turn your anger inward. This is how a public relations man feels about his self-anger:

> I had a great job with one of the best firms in New York. I could have been a vice president by now. But I blew it. I didn't see what was happening until it was too late. Why couldn't I get straight sooner, before I lost it all? Why was I so blind, so stubborn?

In the past, he would have smoked cocaine to cope with anger. Now, in recovery, he recognizes that anger hurts his recovery and damages work relationships. What can he do? Three techniques may work in controlling anger:

1. Awareness training can help you identify episodes that trigger anger. A counselor or therapist can help you list incidents that make you most angry, somewhat angry, and least angry. Then he or she can guide you through the process of systematic desensitization, dealing with events from least anger-provoking to most. You learn to fully feel the anger and deal with it through such methods as deep breathing, meditation, visualization, and imaging. You learn to vent anger through energy-releasing exercise and recreation, not hostility.

2. Assertiveness training can help you deal with anger-provoking people or situations. You learn to identify what you want and to express it clearly, in a manner that promotes cooperation, instead of retaliation.

3. Compassion and understanding help you see the other person's viewpoint. As you make progress in your recovery, you may better understand others' behavior. If you can look past a person's words and actions and understand the reasons behind them, you will judge less and empathize more. Then you will make a great step forward; you will turn that compassion and understanding within, toward yourself.

One of the most liberating feelings you can have is allowing yourself to be human, complete with stupid mistakes, faulty thinking, fierce defenses, inflated ego, and low self-worth.

Joy

Relief, freedom, and gratitude for recovery can lift your emotions to a joyful peak. But you may be afraid of your joy, because in your addictive past, joy always turned into despair. But, with time in recovery, you will come to a comfortable acceptance that keeps you balanced and confident.

Frank Griffin, Administrative Director of the Bishop Gooden Home, a halfway house in Pasadena, California, had this experience with emotional ups and downs:

> When I was two years sober, I started a drunk-driving program in Pasadena. It was the first one, and now it's a big to-do in the state. I worked eight months to put it together, on my own time, and I had all the departments cooperating — the Department of Transportation, the Probation Department, the Highway Patrol, the Automobile Club — they were all behind me. But it wasn't going to work unless the judge approved it. When I had everything finalized and had the letters of support, I sent the whole package to the presiding judge. My friends and I took the judge to lunch, to get his opinion, and he pumped me with questions. Finally he said, "Frank, it's a go. I'll have to talk to the other judges, but I'm sure it's okay."
>
> As we were walking out, my friends asked me, "Aren't you excited?" I said, "I'm glad, but I haven't gone to that high peak." In the past, when something big would happen — a big promotion or a successful project — that used to put me on a high. This time, I didn't get there. And I don't think I would have gone down to the low if he would have said no.
>
> I was, nonetheless, concerned about my feelings. I thought I should be jumping up and down. I meditated at

home and tried to figure what was going on with me. Was I sick or what? But then the realization finally hit me. It took me all that night to figure out that I had grown emotionally. I could accept the yes or the no. Emotionally, I could accept that not everything would go my way. I thought, *You finally grew up, stupid. You can accept it, good or bad, and you don't have to go way up or way down.* I can roll along, nice and easy, like waves. I can handle it now.

Let me give you a few tips on how to handle joy. First, enjoy good feelings. You have been sick and desperate long enough. But don't let your elation push you into a situation you may later regret. For example, you may be tempted to preach the clean and sober life to friends and co-workers or run out and make amends to everyone you have ever known. These actions are basically good ones, but they may not be wise during early sobriety. You may meet strong resistance if you try to change the world by next Thursday.

Take time to learn more about your new clean and sober life, to make supportive friends, and to work your program a step at a time. After a while, your emotions will smooth out and you will be better able to handle life's pleasures with equanimity.

Moderating your emotions can not only encourage a quality recovery, it can also help prevent relapse. Elation, the emotional high, can lead to relapse because drinking or using seems the natural way to celebrate. Joy should be enjoyed, but not flaunted. It should be moderated, but not muffled. It should be appreciated, but not to excess.

WHO NEEDS TO KNOW?

When you come back from treatment, does anybody need to know? When you a join a support group or begin an outpatient program, should you discuss your decision with your boss or co-workers? What about anonymity? Wouldn't it be better to keep this matter to yourself?

Several people at work may already know. If you entered treatment through the company's EAP, your EAP counselor knows and your immediate supervisor may also know. Besides, your co-workers are no dumbies. You were gone several weeks; they knew you had problems. Depending on how adeptly or clumsily you hid your addiction, they can easily figure out where you have been. They probably are not going to buy your "I've been on vacation" story.

What, if anything, should you tell them? Recovering people, counselors, psychologists, physicians, and support groups suggest three different approaches.

Tell No One

Some experts feel that the fewer people who know, the better. "You don't want a lot of people in the workplace involved in your personal business," says Bobby Sykes, Ph.D., a behavioral consultant. "You cannot manage other people's attitudes."

If no one knows, keep it that way. Or tell only your EAP counselor and/or one management-level person. That one should probably be your boss. If your boss already knows, you might as well be honest with him or her. If he or she does not know, however, resist revealing your situation, especially if the workplace is generally unsympathetic.

Even when an EAP functions effectively within a company, its influence may be limited to certain departments. EAP philosophies may not filter up to top management, and EAP policies may not be implemented or enforced. Your department or division head may be hostile toward you if you reveal your recovery. Steve, an account executive with a stock brokerage firm, told his office manager that he was recovering from cocaine addiction. The next day, Steve's portfolio was removed and given to another broker, his desk was cleared, and his job was gone. No recovering person is immune from the repercussions of telling the right thing to the wrong person.

If your employer thinks alcoholism or drug addiction is a matter of choice or a moral weakness; if your boss or supervisor has suffered from living with an alcoholic or addict; if previous addicted employees have caused trouble for the company; if the presence of an alcoholic or addict could mean loss of business or prestige; if the employer's own addiction is threatened, you can expect anger, resentment, and overt or covert career sabotage.

The "tell no one" approach saves you from such reactions. Others believe this close-mouthed approach can create extreme tension. You worry and wait for others to find out — what will they think? What will you say? This uncertainty can add more pressure to an already pressure-packed recovery. If stress builds up, it can lead to relapse.

Tell Everyone

The "tell everyone" advocates recommend honest, good-natured disclosure. Tell everyone; then you won't have to worry about someone unexpectedly finding out. One recovering alcoholic, an executive recruiter who now runs his own personnel agency, tells how he did it:

> When I sobered up, I made it a point to call client companies and tell them what I was going through and what I was doing about myself. In every case, they accepted it.
>
> Everyone I deal with knows I'm in alcoholism recovery. I don't care *what* people think as long as they're not getting the wrong picture of me. I've got to be honest with them.
>
> I became more successful because I accepted other people's help, and I think that has a lot to do with it — how you feel about yourself and being able to accept the goodwill and help of others.

44

This approach works best when others in the organization have been through treatment and established a good track record. It also works when you and your boss have a close enough relationship that you can talk heart-to-heart. It is a good approach when your job is hanging by a thread (disclosure might stop the firing process) or your reputation as a troublemaker is known throughout the company (honesty might get you a second chance).

Tell Only Those Who Need to Know

A third approach suggests disclosure on a need-to-know basis. First, consider whether your outside support system can adequately handle your work pressures. Can you discuss work issues with your family, friends, sponsor, clergyperson, counselor, aftercare or support group? Or do you need someone at work with whom you can share everyday frictions and frustrations?

Second, consider the reason for each person's interest. When someone asks, "Where have you been for the past six weeks?" or "What's been happening lately?" evaluate the question's depth. Listen to the spoken question, then hear the *unspoken* question. The person's tone and body language will tell you if it is a casual question or a serious concern. You can gauge your response accordingly. An offhand remark usually needs no lengthy explanation, but your office mate's sincere probing may warrant a deep, closed-door discussion. Look for persons who really want to know. They offer you an opportunity to leave your fear and shame and to share your newly found perspectives.

You have the power to set the tone. Says Frances Lee Menlove, Ph.D., Chief Psychologist and head of the EAP at Los Alamos National Laboratory:

> What other people say and think depends about ninety percent on how you act. You are very powerful in that regard. By the way you approach others, how outgoing

45

you are, you set the stage for how others think about you. The power isn't with the group, it's with the individual.

Others will catch the clues you throw. If you sneak into the office, close your door, and hide out all day, you are throwing out "shame" vibrations. But if you want others to respond to you in a positive way, rehearse positive statements and behaviors that will elicit that response. The following answers give co-workers a positive frame of reference:

- "I was in a treatment center, and it was a remarkable experience."
- "I decided to do something about my drinking, and I feel great about it."
- "I'm going to an outpatient treatment program. It was a hard decision, but now I'm starting to feel the benefits."
- "I never thought I'd wind up in a halfway house. But, you know, it's given me a whole new outlook on life."

What if you tell someone the truth and he or she responds with anger or disapproval? Then you have found out an important fact: that person does not value your doing something to help yourself. Do you want a relationship with that kind of person? From now on, you must select and qualify people, looking for those who value your decision, the recovery process, and your honesty and courage.

When you identify such people, you can go to them for accurate feedback. "Reality testing" means checking your perceptions and feelings (somewhat the worse for wear after the emotional upheaval of early recovery) with a reliable person. Ask your boss if your interpersonal skills are improving. Accept his or her evaluation and make corrections if needed. These kinds of actions help you overcome low self-confidence.

The question of whom to tell also involves your self-esteem. You are who you are. When you pretend to be Mr. or Ms. Perfect, you appear stiff, unfriendly, phony. When you feel comfortable with your real self, others feel comfortable around you. At some time in your recovery, you will want to grow into a new level of self-acceptance. In that higher state, you can pursue your own values, develop intimacy with selected co-workers, and confidently do what you know is right for you. Here's how K. J., an electronics engineer, accepted himself and increased his self-esteem.

I went to treatment in January 1986. I was afraid to face the other employees, not my boss, because he was the one who helped me get in there. I was worried about how I'd be received when I got back. I didn't want to be labeled. The treatment center told me that it was my own problem, that I had to accept it and live with it — the hell with what other people thought. I couldn't expect others to understand because they hadn't been there.

The people in my office knew what was going on and were glad to see me back. They'd ask questions and I'd answer them truthfully. They were satisfied. Some of my other co-workers had an idea, but they didn't bring it up and I didn't either. If they had a need to know, then I'd tell them.

Now I'm taking care of myself, realizing I'm worth more. Before, I was withdrawn, didn't talk much. People were put off. Today I'm a lot more open. In my own office, I talk about my disease. Sometimes I sing to release what I'm thinking and express what I'm feeling. Today, that's okay.

❈ ❈ ❈ ❈ ❈

Many of us are not accustomed to dealing with our emotions. No one encouraged us to express our feelings and no one we knew talked about emotions. We forgot we had them. Now they may be too much for us to handle alone. While trusted family members, friends, and co-workers can listen and empathize, they may be unable to offer the guidance we need to make needed corrections. We may need to look for professional help. That's fine. We don't have to tough this out alone. In fact, the "I can handle this myself" attitude is very unrealistic. According to Robert Meyers:

> Drinking behavior is the tip of the iceberg. Eighty to ninety percent of the problems lie beneath the surface. All the problems that underlie the drinking will not dissipate quickly. It takes hard work, sensitivity, therapy, and time. That's why outpatient programs, aftercare programs, and self-help groups are important to recovery, because recovery does not happen overnight.

This transitional stage is a shaky, scary time, full of new experiences. Feeling unsure of yourself, you are in danger of falling back on old behaviors, and you already know those don't work. To help you deal with your emotions, you might benefit from talking to an addictions counselor, mental health therapist, psychologist, or other trained professional to get all the help and support you need.

ENDNOTES
Chapter Two

1. Carole Hyatt and Linda Gottlieb, *When Smart People Fail* (New York: Penguin Books, 1988), 131.

2. D. Baskin and C. Missouri, "A Treatment Outcome Study of Alcohol Halfway House Residents in the South Bronx," *International Journal of the Addictions* 18 (1983): 552.

3. W. B. Braunstein et al., "Employment Factors in Outpatient Recovery of Alcoholics: A Multivariate Study," *Addictive Behaviors*/8 (1983) 348.

4. Richard B. Seymour and David E. Smith, *Drugfree* (New York: Facts On File Publications, 1987), 14.

5. Deborah L. Rhoads, "A Longitudinal Study of Life Stress and Social Support Among Drug Abusers," *International Journal of the Addictions* 18 (1983): 206.

6. Ellen Schultz, "Giving Employees a Helping Hand," *EAP Digest* (March/April 1988): 17.

TOWARD A HEALTHY WORK LIFE

Everyone wants to be fit and healthy. Our national interest in fitness and health pours billions of dollars into spa membership, exercise equipment, workout clothing, aerobics classes and tapes, and nutritional supplements to give us that healthy glow.

Alcoholics and other addicts who are drinking or using drugs want to look fit and healthy too. They think if they look healthy, rested, relaxed, alert, and coordinated, they cannot possibly be sick with an addictive disease. A healthy appearance can be an excuse to continue the addiction that is destroying their health, as well as a cover-up for those who might be watching. They may jog religiously seven days a week, play tennis on weekends, play handball or racquetball with clients, work out with weights or machines, and take enough vitamins and mineral supplements to make their pharmacist rich, but still not be healthy.

They may soak up the sun's rays or lie under tanning machines to get rid of paleness. They may use eye drops for swelling and redness, mouthwash for stale breath, and makeup for facial lines and body bruises. They can hide the surface ravages of addiction. But inside, their body pays a terrible price.

Nutritionally, they starve their body. A practicing alcoholic thinks he is healthy when he munches peanuts while downing his eighth martini. Or a using addict thinks she is healthy when she remembers to eat at all. Or they may think that health foods and vitamins protect them from the harm that other abusers suffer. They may try the "Vitamin Cure" or the "Health Farm Cure," hoping a few days of recuperation will restore them to health and let them drink or use with their former zest.

In reality, alcoholics and addicts suffer tremendous physical deterioration. All of the body is affected.[1] The body organs, nervous system, immune system, circulatory system — the cells that compose the body's structure — are damaged. Some alcoholics have irreparable liver and brain damage. Cocaine users may face blood pressure problems and increased heartbeat, leading to ventricular tachycardia, excessive weight loss, and impotency.

Those who use drugs intravenously are prone to infections of the blood and skin, Acquired Immune Deficiency Syndrome (AIDS), and dead or gangrenous tissue where the drug was injected. Women drug users, particularly, may develop urinary tract infections.[2] Poor hygiene, a rundown condition, and lack of effective health practices make drug users easy prey for colds, flu, or any other infection.

TIME HEALS

While some damage cannot be repaired (the liver, for example, may not fully repair itself), most can be completely reversed *in time*. For recovering people, six months to two years of abstinence may be needed to repair nervous system damage and complete other repair work.[3, 4]

Psychological and emotional recovery may take longer. Prescription drugs, particularly the sedative/tranquilizer benzodiazepines (Valium, Librium, Xanax, Tranxene, Centrax, and Ativan, to name a few), can disrupt mental processes for long periods after detoxification. Jaynee Parnegg, now Vice President of Jim Kelly Counseling Associates, says that her physical recovery from Valium took almost three years.

Jaynee was active in Alcoholics Anonymous and the National Council on Alcoholism, operating her own flower business, when her doctor prescribed Valium to relieve stomach cramps caused by old scar tissue. A small, four-milligram dose every day would be "nonaddicting," or so both Jaynee and her doctor thought.

Valium unsettled Jaynee's thought processes so much she thought she was losing her mind. It affected her judgment. She couldn't figure out how many flowers to order and ended up ordering too many, throwing them out, and losing money. It affected her short-term memory and ability to verbalize her thoughts. "My brain was functioning," she says, "but I couldn't get what I was thinking from my brain to my mouth." Valium brought on sudden, vicious anxiety attacks. She felt woozy, unsteady on her feet, and unsteady in her mind.

After treatment for Valium withdrawal, Jaynee says, "I'd have anxiety attacks when there was no reason to feel anxious. I was sometimes tired, forgetful, and disoriented. If someone criticized me, I would take it in an exaggerated sense. My life seemed slightly out of focus, about one bubble off. Six months later, I felt fine, but I was still noticing symptoms years later."

Here is the point: Even low levels of alcohol or other drugs can damage you. Your body needs time to repair itself. You may feel better than you have felt in years, thanks to abstinence, good nutrition, education, and support. But your body, mind, and spirit need time to heal. If you were recovering from a serious accident or surgery, you would need to gain strength and stabilize your body. Even after months of progress, you would make sure your physical condition did not aggravate the psychological or emotional stress of returning to work.[5] Your recovery from a near-fatal addiction must be handled just as carefully.

Recovering persons set high expectations for themselves. They want to be well *right now*. They want to make up for lost time and get their career back on track *today*. They may rush to the workplace and try to regain peak performance immediately. Usually, the body and mind rebel, emotions flare, and their recovery is endangered. Instead, try not to blame yourself if you cannot work as efficiently as you think you should. Give yourself a break. Apply the Twelve Step program slogan, Easy Does It to each activity. You will gain strength and stamina, energy and stability, one day at a time.

RECOVERING YOUR HEALTH

Most people leave treatment for addiction in better condition than when they entered. But even if you chose not to go through treatment, your program of abstinence and group support will soon have you feeling healthier than you've felt in a long time.

Nevertheless, you can expect some physical problems to follow you back to work. If you know what to expect, you can apply liberal doses of patience and program. Physical problems needn't throw you back into old, harmful behaviors. Also, you can alert appropriate persons at work and ask for their help when needed. Here are some physical problems you may face.

Low Energy, Fatigue

Some recovering people feel tired and lack energy for days or weeks into recovery. Or they may have periods when they feel overwhelmingly fatigued. Exhaustion may come minutes before an important meeting, during a big sales presentation, or while you are trying to beat a deadline. According to Gary L. Simpson, M.D., former Medical Director of Presbyterian Hospital Alcohol and Drug Treatment Center, it takes time to recover from long-term toxicity.

"If alcohol was your drug of choice, it may have damaged muscles," says Dr. Simpson. "Long-term exposure can weaken the major muscles of the thighs, upper arms, and proximal muscle groups. Muscular damage from the effects of alcohol takes time to repair and regain strength. To think that you will not be fatigued for some time is probably unrealistic. Clinically, we see this condition more commonly in women than men."

You may want to discuss your physical condition with your boss and co-workers and assure them that the fatigue is temporary. Ordinarily, your energy level will return as your recovery progresses.

Look at your work practices to see where you might use some energy-saving techniques. For example, you might communicate by telephone or intercom, rather than leaving your desk. You might decrease the noise surrounding your area (noise can be very tiring). You might ask others to help you complete a task. You may need to rest your head on your desk for five minutes now and then. Or, instead of coming in early and staying late, work regular hours.

Fatigue is normal. Normal people get tired. But tiredness can also be a symptom of something else. Your fatigue may be mostly psychological, an effect from an earlier "pink cloud" period. Or it may indicate more serious problems, such as depression or physical illness. Give yourself a few weeks to get back to your normal energy level. If fatigue continues, see a physician who understands addiction and in whom you can confide. For heaven's sake, don't self-medicate!

Medication Sensitivity

Many recovering persons, particularly newly clean narcotics users, may be hypersensitive to pain. Their body's ability to produce pain-reducing substances has been damaged.[6] Yet, recovering people who take pain-reducing medication risk relapse into addiction. They cannot safely take any prescribed or over-the-counter medication that contains an addictive substance, such as codeine, Demerol, or alcohol. While AA warns strongly against *ever* taking such medications, many physicians and counselors add the qualification, *unless necessary to control a serious or life-threatening health condition.* Then, *with the supervision of an addiction-experienced physician and counselor*, appropriate medications can be taken.

Dr. George Nash, Medical Director of Sierra Tucson Treatment Center, gives this helpful advice for using medications:

> We use medicine only when absolutely necessary, when natural ways aren't working. Tension headaches, for example, respond to stress-reducing biofeedback, relaxation techniques, working the Steps with your sponsor, doing anger therapy. These are much better than taking a pill.
>
> When medicine is necessary, the best rule is this: Use it when there is no other method or alternative that is more natural. It's perfectly proper. Narcotics can be used for acute pain. If I have my gall bladder out, I'm going to have a shot of morphine post-operatively. But my sponsor is going to know, and my physician is going to know that I'm chemically dependent.

Sleep Disorders

For most people, not getting a good night's sleep ruins the whole day. You need to look wide awake and alert for an early morning meeting, yet not even four cups of coffee can shake away the cobwebs. Simply the fear of not sleeping, not being fresh for tomorrow's obligations, can keep you from falling asleep.

Many chemically dependent people suffer from sleep disorders. In fact, drug dependency is the third leading cause of insomnia.[7] Insomnia, frequent awakenings during the night, disrupted sleep cycles, and terrifying nightmares create anxiety and exhaustion.

In the early stages of addiction, higher levels of drugs would induce sleep. But eventually the drugs no longer helped. Instead, they created even more serious sleep problems, cycles of sleeping and waking that were constantly disturbed and anxiety-provoking.

In recovery, sleep often continues to be a problem, sometimes temporary, sometimes lifelong.[8] You may have trouble falling asleep, then find yourself waking frequently. You may have weird, vivid dreams that awaken you or prevent deep rest. Your sleep patterns may change; for example, you may need less or more sleep than usual. Fortunately, these problems usually decrease as months of abstinence increase.

All addictive substances profoundly affect sleep patterns, especially rapid eye movement (REM) sleep, the dreaming portion of sleep that is essential for restfulness. Dr. Simpson says, "For individuals that may not be able to remember a non-sedated night's sleep in the previous weeks, months, or decades, it is not unexpected that they would have difficulty reestablishing normal sleep/wake cycles."

Before most persons leave treatment, their sleep patterns become more regular. Those in outpatient programs or support groups can expect to sleep better after approximately thirty days of abstinence. According to Dr. Nash, however, sleep patterns may take a year after treatment for REM sleep to return to normal.

Some recovering persons may have a primary sleep disorder, aside from their chemical dependency. Because of bouts with insomnia, you may have started drinking alcoholically or using sedative drugs to help you sleep. Then you became addicted to the substance. When you begin abstaining, the primary sleep disorder may return. In that case, you may need to consult a sleep disorder psychologist or psychiatrist who understands addiction. When the underlying cause is treated, insomnia usually diminishes significantly or disappears.

For the name of a certified addictionologist in your city or area, contact your city medical society, state medical association, a local office of the National Council on Alcoholism, or a local hospital referral service.

Sleep disorders must be taken seriously. Like fatigue, they may be a symptom of another medical problem, such as primary endogenous depression. Untreated, sleep disorders can set a recovering person up for relapse. For most recovering alcoholics and addicts, however, sleep soon becomes the blessing it was intended to be.

You can help improve your sleep patterns by following these suggestions:

1. *Establish consistent sleep habits.* Sleep in the same bed in the same room, and go to bed at the same time every night. Don't do anything but *sleep* in your bed. If you want to read reports or sketch ideas, go into another room.

2. *Reduce or eliminate caffeine or any medications that may affect your sleep.* Watch your reactions to over-the-counter medications, and avoid those that make you wakeful.

3. *Keep your bedroom cool and dark.* Cut down on outside noise with earplugs. If your dog or cat sleeps on your bed, you may need to exile your animal friend until good sleep returns.

4. *Don't eat before bedtime.* The stomach's digestive process can keep you awake. If you must have a snack, avoid fibrous foods, such as apples, which take time to digest. Also avoid sugar products, such as soft drinks and cookies, since sugar can elevate your blood sugar level and keep you wakeful.

5. *Exercise regularly*, not just on weekends, but not immediately before bedtime.

Memory and Coordination Problems

Wouldn't it be wonderful if we could walk through a door marked *Recovery* and emerge completely cured? We could immediately go back to work looking better, feeling stronger, and performing better than ever. We would feel good about ourselves and our new life. Instant wellness would be wonderful, but even if you escape fatigue, low energy, and sleep disorders, you will probably get hit with another symptom.

One of the most exasperating problems in your recovery may be inability to think quickly and clearly. For career persons who must make instant decisions or recall information accurately, this symptom may cause frustration. Your intelligence has not been affected, but you may be unable to concentrate on what others are saying or doing, or you may lose your train of thought in the middle of a conversation.

You may have short-term memory loss; that is, you cannot immediately recall your boss's name or the next portion of your speech. You may not remember yesterday's meeting or last week's conference. When you cannot remember quickly or clearly, you must relearn today what you learned yesterday. Therefore, learning new skills and information becomes more difficult.[9]

Memory retraining may help, and memory ticklers like making lists and keeping an appointment calendar help you remember. But the only known cure is time. A sense of humor and patience with yourself help too. Be grateful that you are getting better, not worse; try to understand and accept what is happening. You needn't feel stupid or ashamed; you will get everything back or make the necessary adjustments in time.

Poor Physical Coordination

Just when you want to appear suave, you knock the telephone off your customer's desk. Be aware that your coordination may be out of whack for a while. You may feel dizzy or off balance. What once were razor-sharp reflexes now seem bedded in quicksand.

These symptoms won't last long. Nevertheless, as a precaution, you may want to cut down your driving, ask for temporary assignment to a less complicated machine, or get an assistant to handle anything that requires physical coordination. (Handling audiovisual materials can be particularly frustrating. Enlist a helper to turn pages, arrange slides, adjust the VCR.) You may want to discuss this condition with your supervisor, or your supervisor may decide to reassign you and monitor your performance until you are ready to resume regular duties.

When to Return to Work

None of these mental and physical problems need keep you away from work. In fact, research and experience indicate that the sooner you return to work, the better your recovery will progress. Returning to work helps us feel normal again. It can have a therapeutic effect, especially in reducing anxieties and negative thinking that may surround returning to work.

Recovering people sometimes fear going back to work. To avoid confronting that fear, they convince themselves they are too sick to work. The longer they stay away from their workplace, the more they believe themselves to be sick. And, of course, sick persons don't work. This kind of thinking can slow your recovery because it delays your return to normal living. It can also cost you customers and income, as in Carl's case.

> After a twenty-eight day treatment program, Carl decided to rest at home. A successful real estate salesman, he believed that he wasn't physically ready to go back to work. His biggest worry focused on his appearance. Although he felt fine, he says, "I didn't look right." Jaundice had turned his skin a sickly yellow, and poor liver function had made him look bloated and paunchy. "Real estate is a very sociable business," he said. "I didn't want my customers to see me looking that way."

> A month in treatment plus a month at home equaled two months out of touch with clients. When he returned to the office, he didn't have a single listing. Two years later, his production is still not back to his previous high, and he worries that his sales manager will find a replacement.

Would Carl have been better off had he returned to work a day or two after treatment? Probably. He looked jaundiced and puffy *before* treatment; why would anyone care *after* treatment? Since his sales manager knew about and approved of Carl's treatment, the manager would have understood a temporary slowdown in production. Carl's customers would have gotten the service they needed, and losses would have been held to a minimum. The delay cost him dearly.

Watch for Physical Warnings

You can expect some physical ups and downs as your recovery rolls along, such as inadequate liver functioning or high blood pressure. Medical intervention may be the only solution. Nonetheless, if you continue to experience fatigue, depression, mental confusion — or any physical problem not normal for you — you should consider these warnings that you need to do something differently.

Listen to your body's messages. Stomachaches, headaches, colds, backaches — or any other manifestation of stress and anxiety — are clues to what is happening in your recovery. "They are important cues to how centered you are, how well you are feeling in your recovery, and what you need to do to avoid setting yourself up for relapse," says Dr. Simpson. "Most importantly, don't ignore them."

STRESS: THE NUMBER ONE ENEMY

Work produces pressure. Showing up five days a week, commuting through rush-hour traffic, meeting deadlines and quotas, dealing with difficult people, and pulling the best out of your abilities — these activities create pressure.

Normal living produces pressure. Your spouse, children, friends, family, plus church and community involvement, can add up to a pressure-filled life.

Recovery creates its own pressure.[10] Outside changes can strain your inner coping skills to the maximum, and you cannot use your old, reliable coping mechanism — alcohol or other drugs. If you are unequipped to adapt to pressure, stress can aggravate emotional, psychological, or physical problems, and vice versa.

Robert Dato, Ph.D., a Philadelphia psychoanalyst who specializes in stress says, "Stress is the *result*, the manifestation of the gap between pressure and adaptability."

When you are under a great deal of pressure and your adaptability is low, your stress will be high. To decrease the stress, you can decrease the pressure, increase your adaptability, or both. Lower pressure with higher adaptability seems the best equation for a healthy recovery.

You know you are undergoing stress when your body, mind, and emotions enter the "flight or fight" pattern. You feel it in your gut. Pressure builds up, causing problems to emerge. Your emotions may start a roller coaster ride. Your concentration and attention span may lapse, or your physical coordination may slip. Unfortunately, recovering persons may not recognize these signals until stress reaches an extreme level.

Stress may also activate destructive compulsions that make you feel worse instead of bringing relief. Under stress, some of us might binge on ice cream or peanut butter as a "reward," then suffer sugar-induced headaches, fatigue, and depression. Others of us might go shopping, spend too much money, then blame ourselves for not having more control. Blame and guilt only increase stress. A high level of stress, untended for a long period, can lead to relapse.

Clearly, stress is dangerous to recovery. Yet, to expect the workplace to be problem free can create even more stress. When you expect that everyone will like, protect, and appreciate you, you set yourself up for disappointment and resentment.

Dr. Menlove says this about expectations:

> Many persons have an incorrect idea about how good the world should act toward them. It should be benign, fair, sensitive, understanding. Then they look around and see the nonsense, the make-work, the things that shouldn't happen, the people who don't do their job. These situations occur in every workplace. It's nice if you can correct them, but to expect an idyllic, stress-free environment is unworkable.

Because stress is so dangerous and so universal, the best solution is to learn to manage it. Stress management is an internal resource,[11] a skill that can be developed. Along with abstinence, support, and balanced living, stress management helps you enjoy a successful career and a fulfilling recovery. It consists of three aspects:

1. Identifying where stress comes from.

2. Taking action to reduce stress.

3. Changing your attitude.

Identifying Where Stress Comes From

In *As Bill Sees It*, Bill W. mentions the term, "trigger event."[12] This is an event or situation that increases pressure and to which you respond by feeling stress. For you, a trigger event might be making a speech to your business association or negotiating a raise. Or, you may feel stress when your boss calls you "honey" or your secretary takes yet another day off.

Normal people suffer stress from such events, but recovering people often overreact because they are "stress sensitive."[13] They translate minor stress into major *dis*tress, and react in an exaggerated way. For example, a canceled appointment (minor stress) may generate explosive anger and indignation, turning to rage (major stress reaction). Without their favorite coping mechanism, alcohol or other drugs, their stress may surface in a wide array of psychosomatic symptoms, including headaches, backaches, hyperventilation, and any of the other reactions already discussed.

Try to identify your trigger events before overreacting. More than likely, these events involve one of three elements.[14]

1. *Other people may upset you.* When you don't get along with your boss, when a co-worker doesn't do his or her job, when you believe you are being used or abused, pressure builds up. A person's work style may conflict with yours, putting you in a state of constant friction.

When I wrote copy for a large Chicago ad agency, my creative supervisor wanted dozens of ideas for every ad. I believed his approach made the agency look tacky and indecisive. I wanted to do one or two excellent pieces of creative work, not a score of mediocre ones.

Obviously, our work styles clashed. Since he headed up my group, I complied with his directions—reluctantly. Because our work styles always collided, every assignment resulted in stress.

2. *Company practices that affect your ability to do your job or get ahead may frustrate you.* Perhaps taking a sick day off reflects badly on your job record; a supervisor arbitrarily assigns overtime; a low budget keeps you from getting needed equipment; or only graduates from the "right" colleges get promoted. While these practices are not written down as formal company or union practices, they nonetheless influence your job and career.

3. *Conditions you cannot control, such as those which are intrinsic to the company or your occupation, may trigger stress.* Examples include seniority, nepotism, noise, quotas, annual reviews, shift work, deadlines, danger, excessive physical exertion, or repetition and boredom. When you cannot change outside circumstances and you are unwilling to change within yourself, pressure can build up and boil over. Your frustration increases when others don't see what you are so upset about.

What triggers stress for you may not trigger stress for me. If it makes *you* tense, nervous, angry, or depressed, then it is a stressor you must deal with, no matter how other people might look at it.

Taking Actions to Reduce Stress

Learning to reduce and control stress can save your career and your recovery. You may want to take a course in stress management training (SMT) through a university or career center. You may want to work one-on-one with your EAP counselor or therapist to learn and rehearse stress management techniques. Or you may want to add some of the following suggestions to your recovery program.

1. Reality testing helps you reinterpret what stresses you.

By interpreting an event from another point of view, the event often loses its stressfulness. Reality testing requires another person to help you test your perceptions. The reality tester should be someone whose opinion and judgment you trust, perhaps your boss or supervisor, your minister, mentor, counselor, or Twelve Step program sponsor. You aren't looking for someone to agree with you. You are looking for someone to check the accuracy of your observations, to suggest an alternate interpretation, and to spot negative thinking and help you make it positive. You want to find the *message* in the experience so you can learn and grow from it.

When Red, the car salesman you met in Chapter One, returned to work after treatment, his boss laid down a new set of rules. Red could never again drive a company car. He must attend AA meetings and keep a signed log to verify his attendance. He must account for his time away from the office. Red resented what he considered unfair restrictions. After all, he had "served his time," hadn't he? Why couldn't he have the same freedoms other salespersons had?

In aftercare sessions, Red tested his reality. He talked about his resentments and got feedback from group members. They reminded Red that, during his last drunk, he had damaged a company car and been arrested for DWI. The dealership had a right to be concerned about his driving. They pointed out that the company had no obligation to rehire Red. He was lucky to have a good job in a place that advocated treatment. Finally, they told Red that he had an advantage over other salespersons — the boss was watching Red's every move. That gave Red a chance to prove what he could do. When someone watches you and sees your progress, you get credit for your achievements.

With reality testing, Red reinterpreted the dealership's attitude. "I realized it was fair, that it was my fault, not theirs. I needed to prove that I could live with their rules, that I could do a good job, that I wasn't washed up." This view took the sting out of the new rules and significantly decreased his stress. Those are big benefits for verbalizing and ventilating your experiences and for listening to and considering other persons' interpretation of reality.

You can also use reality testing to evaluate how you come across to others. You may think you appear nervous or sound stupid. Ask someone. You may think your comments or suggestions were poorly received. Ask someone. Often, your self-consciousness makes you perceive a disaster where there is only a minor setback. Ask someone how he or she saw the incident, and watch how his or her comments cut the matter down to manageable size.

2. "A" does not equal "C" is a new concept for recovering persons.

Most of us think that a stressful event must automatically bring about a stress reaction. When an "A" event happens (flat tire), we get a "C" reaction (headache). Here are some typical "A" events and "C" reactions you might experience.

"A" event	*...causes...*	*"C" reaction*
Car won't start		*stomach upset*
Kids are whiny		*backache*
Boss is grouchy		*nervousness*
Unreasonable deadline		*irritability*
Check bounces		*shouting*
Misfiled information		*losing temper*

In recovery, we must learn that "A" does not equal "C." We can increase our adaptability and lower our stress level by implementing "B."

Dr. Menlove urges, "Break into the automatic thinking that says, 'A broken-down car makes me upset.' Or, 'My boss did this, therefore I'm frustrated.' 'A' does not equal 'C.' It must go through 'B.' 'B' is where you think about it and interpret it. Get off the notion that your actions have to reflect the way you feel. Your actions should be focused on the desired outcome."

First, she suggests, get rid of all the "A's" you can. If you cannot get rid of a stressor, try changing the way you look at it (reinterpreting). Then bring out the "B's" to help you interrupt the automatic reaction and bring a positive outcome.

"B" actions
Going to a Twelve Step meeting
Aerobic exercise
Good nutrition
Prayer, meditation
Relaxation tapes
Reading spiritual literature
Doing something nice for yourself
Talking to a friend or sponsor
Laughing it off
Enjoying your hobby

Add to the "B's" any other actions that work for you. When a stressful event happens, stop yourself from automatically reacting. Instead, plug in a "B" action. You will immediately lower your stress level, think more clearly, and get more enjoyment from your work.

3. Taking care of your body pays big dividends in stress reduction.

Many of us don't exercise, or we believe being thin means being healthy. We need to learn new eating habits that reduce stress and promote recovery. We need to establish a comfortable, enjoyable exercise program to give us a sense of well-being and self-confidence. When we fail to take care of ourselves, stress may build up because our body's functions break down.[15]

What you put in your mouth can increase stress. If it has mood-altering qualities, it can become a factor in relapse. For some people, sugar causes uncomfortable mood swings.[16] From twenty to sixty minutes after eating that luscious apple turnover, the "sugar high" drops, leaving you tired, fuzzy-headed, and irritable. Some people get a sugar-induced headache and sugar cravings after eating just one dish of ice cream.

If you are affected negatively, avoid any food or beverage that contains sugar. This rule eliminates most desserts and candy, some fruit juices, most soft drinks, many brands of peanut butter, and most ice cream. Be careful with other sugars, such as honey, molasses, and syrup. Also be on your guard against dried fruits and raisins, since these contain concentrated natural sugars.

This no-sugar rule means rethinking your meals. No more quick orange-juice-and-sweet-roll breakfasts. No more candy bars on your afternoon coffee break. Instead, increase your intake of grains, such as whole grain breads and cereals; eat more fruits and vegetables and fewer animal products, especially red meats; cut down on preserved and processed foods, such as hot dogs, bologna, canned vegetables and meats, and frozen dinners; and add more legumes (beans, peas, lentils, peanuts) and seeds and nuts to your diet.

Caffeine, like sugar, demands a high price for a momentary lift. That wake-up cup of coffee, along with additional coffee breaks throughout the day, can push you into a nervous state. They can make you feel edgy and irritable all day and restless and wakeful all night. Switching to decaffeinated coffee and soft drinks can start a personal battle (the taste *is* different, no matter what the commercials say), but it arms you with another weapon against stress.

What you don't put in your mouth can produce stress too. Don't let yourself go too long without food. Hunger stresses the body and makes you think erratically. Eat a good breakfast; give your body a balanced lunch.

Dieting stresses your body because it is not getting its normal supply of calories, even if those calories were more than it needed. Then, if you fall off your diet, you feel guilty and ashamed, which adds more stress. Early sobriety is not the best time to start a diet. Get yourself on a healthy, balanced nutritional plan with adequate calories. Later, when you are comfortably back to work and firmly into recovery, consider a weight-loss program.

Not lighting up a cigarette creates a different kind of hunger, a craving that can be extremely stressful. Nicotine is a highly addictive, mood-altering substance. As long as it is in your system, you are not really drug free. You are still addicted to a substance that can kill you. Quitting smoking is one of the best things you can do for your health and your recovery. When you are ready to quit, you will reap a lifetime of healthful benefits.

Exercise is another healthful practice that is good for your recovery. Regular exercise improves your health, your sense of well-being, and your ability to handle stress. Many studies show that aerobic exercise (running, walking, swimming, bicycling) particularly benefits recovering persons.[17, 18]

At Haight Ashbury Free Medical Clinics in San Francisco, running is prescribed as a way to reduce drug hunger during early recovery.[19] Some doctors and psychologists say that the neurochemical change caused by exercise helps counter the negative changes from drugs, including nicotine or food. Others credit beta blockers and neurotransmitters with producing benefits from lowered cholesterol to greater contentment.

If you have come to a stage in your recovery where nothing seems to be happening, you can get yourself moving with a daily exercise program. It is a self-improving *action* that can change the way you think about yourself. A better attitude always opens up new opportunities for growth, both in your career and in your recovery.

Other stress reducers include prayer, meditation, biofeedback, yoga, deep breathing, acupuncture, sauna, and hydrotherapy. Good, old-fashioned fun and play probably qualify as the best stress reducers of all. One or more of these methods will combine well with your nutrition and exercise program — but none should replace it.

Personally, I prefer stress reducers I can use wherever I am. I can never tell when stress will boil over into an anxiety attack, anger, or tears. To keep stress from building to the boiling point, I begin my day with a half-hour of low-impact aerobics. Then I do relaxation stretches wherever I can find enough space (women's room, airplane aisle, waiting area). I use meditation with visualization, plus deep breathing, to lower my blood pressure and calm my nerves.

Visualizing a beautiful, tranquil place where I am completely safe reminds me that my peace is *within me*. Meditating on the infinite power of my Divine Friend reassures me that I am not alone. Remembering to pray for someone else puts my problems back in perspective. Reading a short spiritual piece stops my mental gyrations and puts me back in the right frame of mind. That right-mindedness is my number one antidote for stress.

4. Setting your own limits helps you reach and maintain an optimum stress level.[20]

You need enough stress to keep you motivated, interested, and productive, but not so much that you become immobilized. When you feel yourself going over your optimum stress level, back off and set a limit. Assertively inform others about your new limit, and be ready to accept their response, good or bad.

Most of us have never thought about our optimum stress level. We push ourselves into situations that don't fit us, then we wonder why we get angry, scared, depressed, or sick. Sometimes we accept a client that is too big for us to handle. Or we agree to finish a project on too tight a timetable. Or we take on another person's job in addition to our own. Or the job we have been hired to do expands to include three more functions. We stretch our resources, trying to become big enough to handle the job. Sometimes we grow. Sometimes we break.

We must be careful not to *set ourselves up for failure*. When we push beyond our optimum stress level, our emotional, psychological, and physical responses kick in. We become anxious, angry, or fearful. Our thinking becomes faulty, confused, and jumbled. We may make ourselves physically ill. Often, we fail miserably unless we stop our behavior, find where we have overreached our limits, and set new ones.

You may not want to look at your limitations, much less reveal them to your superiors. You may not want to set new limits because you are afraid the company will misinterpret your actions. But most organizations want you to focus on doing the best job you possibly can. If your performance can improve under a new set of circumstances, how can they say no?

You should not be expected to work beyond your optimum stress level for any extended length of time. Occasionally, to meet a short-term emergency, you can stand the pressure. But as a daily condition of the workplace, stress is harmful to your health and to your recovery.

Learn to listen to your body. It may be giving you stress signals. If you cannot sleep because your mind is racing, if you lose interest in sex or wreck your car, stress may be the culprit.

Look for places where you can set your own limits. You may need to work with a different team, change your work area, get an assistant or better piece of equipment, close the shop earlier, see fewer patients, or do less personal contact. Whatever keeps you working at or under your optimum stress level is worth the inconvenience or embarrassment of speaking up.

❅ ❅ ❅ ❅ ❅

The problem may be your attitude. You may already be doing everything suggested in this chapter and still feel lousy. The hard-to-define quality of mental attitude contributes more to recovery than any other factor. Whether the disease is alcoholism, another addiction, heart trouble, diabetes, arthritis, or cancer, it usually responds to an attitude of hope, faith, gratitude, humility, self-respect, and self-love. One recovering physician explains the importance of attitude this way:

> Many disabilities are located above the shoulders and between the ears. It's an attitude more than a condition. Recovering persons are prone to shame and guilt. In treatment they work with those issues and hopefully they don't become prolonged problems.
>
> The most important thing to good health is changing that attitude, and that is what AA is all about. I, for example, have hypertension, high blood fats, and arthri-

tis of the hip. I was on three medications for my high blood pressure with only marginal effect. My serum was still turbid, I didn't eat anything except skinned chicken and baked fish for two years, and the arthritis of the hip required medication.

I got on the [AA] program, quit fighting myself, quit fighting life, stayed sober one day at a time, and my blood pressure is normal, my blood fats are normal, I eat what I want. My hip is worse, but I have very little pain and take no medication for that.

The first step to good health is to change an attitude. I am convinced that most diseases come from fighting yourself and fighting life.

ENDNOTES
Chapter Three

1. Richard B. Seymour and David E. Smith, *Drugfree* (New York: Facts on File Publications, 1987), 104.

2. Ibid., 86.

3. James R. Milam and Katherine Ketcham, *Under the Influence* (Seattle, Wash.: Madrona Publishers, 1981), 140.

4. Terence T. Gorski and Merlene Miller, *Staying Sober* (Independence, Mo.: Independence Press, 1986), 58.

5. Milam and Ketcham, *Under the Influence*, 131.

6. Seymour and Smith, *Drugfree*, 172.

7. Milton K. Erman, M.D., "An Overview of Sleep and Insomnia," *Hospital Practice* 23 (Supplement 2, September 1988): 10.

8. Gorski and Miller, *Staying Sober*, 62.

9. Ibid., 60-61.

10. Ibid., 58.

11. D. J. Rohsenow, R. E. Smith, and S. Johnson, "Stress Management Training as a Prevention Program for Heavy Social Drinkers: Cognitive, Affect, Drinking, and Individual Differences," *Addictive Behaviors* 10 (1985): 52.

12. Bill W., "Getting Off a 'Dry Bender,'" *As Bill Sees It* (New York: Alcoholics Anonymous World Services, Inc.), 30.

13. Gorski and Miller, *Staying Sober*, 54.

14. Jack Santa-Barbara and Margaret Coshan, "When the Workplace Is the Cause of Stress. . .," *EAP Digest* (March/April, 1988): 40.

15. Seymour and Smith, *Drugfree*, 104.

16. Milam and Ketcham, *Under the Influence*, 140.

17. T. J. Murphy, R. R. Pagano, and G. A. Marlatt, "Lifestyle Modifications with Heavy Alcohol Drinkers: Effects of Aerobic Exercise and Meditation," *Addictive Behaviors* 11 (1986): 185.

18. Seymour and Smith, *Drugfree*, 151.

19. Ibid., 153.

20. Gorski and Miller, *Staying Sober*, 80.

CHAPTER FOUR

FACING REALITY

Many recovering people see a sweet, sentimental mist covering reality. They have discovered a new way of life, and they expect everyone else to appreciate it as much as they do. In treatment and aftercare programs, counseling sessions and support group meetings, they speak in rapturous tones of their returning health, renewed relationships, newly found spiritual awareness, and inner peace. But the *real world* — the world outside those comforting rooms — can toss many stumbling blocks onto the Road of Happy Destiny. [1]

These obstacles need not stop you. But, if you are not expecting them, they may throw you off balance. Like a good business-person, you want to be prepared for contingencies. What are some unexpected obstacles?

- Lack of communication
- Poor social skills
- Late hits
- Discrimination
- Financial problems

LACK OF COMMUNICATION

Other recovering people understand perfectly what you mean when you talk about your recovery, accepting an unpleasant circumstance, or letting go of a person or situation. But some non-recovering persons will think your remarks are irritating, impractical, even slightly demented. A recovering person saying "recovery is my first priority" to his or her boss may sound like a Sixties flower child saying "make love, not war" to a five-star general!

Other people will not easily understand the incredible conversion experience you have had. When you think, feel, and behave like a new person, you naturally want to share your new way of life with others. Many co-workers, however, will not care about what happened to you. They want to continue making money and getting ahead — that is their reality. Terms like *powerlessness*, *acceptance*, and *spirituality* may as well be a foreign language.

Your boss may squirm uncomfortably when you talk about recovery principles. Recovery concepts, such as "Do the footwork, and everything will turn out the way it should," drive many department heads crazy. Say "Easy Does It" to a hassled line supervisor and watch him explode. The ideas you heard in treatment or counseling often fall on deaf ears in the workplace. Even *recovering bosses* may not want to hear a program slogan when a crisis crashes. Confrontations, misunderstandings, and arguments usually result when you and non-recovering persons tune into different wave lengths.

They may misunderstand your motives. When you entered treatment, they perhaps thought you were looking for a free vacation or were covering up your mistakes. If you seek a calmer work environment, they may think you are lazy, unmotivated, or not a team player. If you say you need less stress, they may resent you and retaliate by excluding you from the information pipeline. Not everyone misunderstands, of course, but enough bosses and peers do that communication barriers can seriously disrupt your working relationships.

What can you do to improve communications? These six suggestions may help.

1. Talk in Their Terms

You cannot communicate with others if you do not speak their language. Recovery terminology will sound foreign to a non-recovering person.

Career persons talk about goals and objectives, team spirit, performance, output, interfacing, productivity, sales, quotas, attitude, cooperation, customer satisfaction, and cost effectiveness. They seldom talk about personal or spiritual growth, unless it is expressed in business jargon. Says Andy Grove, president and chief executive officer of Intel Corporation, in *One-on-One with Andy Grove:*

> How well we communicate is determined not by how well we say things but by how well we are understood. We must have a good measure of our audience — their background, their mood, and their attentiveness. While we can't change any of these, as communicators we *can* and *must* tailor our message so it's appropriate.[2]

But, you don't have to talk gobbledygook. You don't have to "play the game" if it makes no sense. Much of modern business communication is nonsense. Memos often contain indirect, confusing, or unnecessary messages, and person-to-person or person-to-group communication may circle problems and avoid issues. In too many organizations, straight talk is rare, and a sincere expression of emotion is considered a breach of good business sense. Organizational consultants Anne Wilson Schaef and Diane Fassel say, "A common statement is, 'Get control of yourself.' There is a general belief that if feelings are expressed, one will be seen as unstable, and this could jeopardize one's security on the job."[3]

2. Find the Right Time and Place

Timing is important in how well others receive your message. The middle of an emergency is not the time to discuss your long-term goals, nor is the men's room the place to talk about spirituality. If you need a heart-to-heart talk with a supervisor, co-worker, or client, find a block of time when neither of you will feel rushed. Select a quiet place where you can close the door and turn off the telephone.

Consider the other person's time pressures; he or she may have only a few minutes to talk. Get to the point. Let him or her know what you want (advice, action, sympathy, a recommendation, cooperation). Take appropriate follow-up steps, such as writing a memorandum or making a telephone call, to let the person know the outcome of your conversation.

3. Build Trust

Says Wayne Wear, Facility Director of Cottonwood de Albuquerque Treatment Center:

> People come out of treatment waving their certificate of completion, expecting others to jump through hoops and deal with them differently. But they must rebuild trust. You build trust by being responsible, fulfilling your job description. Before, you manipulated and connived. Now you have got to play it straight, be up front with those who need to know, and change negative reactions into positives.

> Building trust means building consistency. Consistency of behavior, attitude, and performance. In the past, your inconsistency may have left others confused and suspicious. When they trusted you, you betrayed that trust, again and again. Now they watch you cautiously, expecting another betrayal. Only steady, consistent trustworthiness rebuilds trust.

4. Contribute

Andy Grove says that diligent and efficient work behind the scenes is no substitute for contributing to an issue while it's being considered and debated.[4]

Speak up. Know the facts and offer workable suggestions. Agree with those whose opinions you support. Disagree only when you have an alternative. Offer a word of wisdom at the right time; it might help.

5. Stop Criticizing and Start Praising

Before you criticize someone's decisions or management style, your co-workers' methods or performance, or the company's ethics or policies, remember that criticism closes ears and shuts doors. No one likes to listen to a bad-mouther, the person who can find nothing good to say.

Offer a word of thanks or appreciation. Recognize another's efforts with a "Nice job." Write a congratulatory note. Buy your team a round of coffee to celebrate a job well done.

6. Ask for Feedback

Communication not only means talking; it means listening. Ask questions to find out how the other person interpreted what you said or did. Did he or she receive your message? Was it clear? Were there any interfering elements, such as interruptions, noise, or equipment failure, that kept the person from getting your message? Are any further details needed? Should you restate the message? Is follow-up communication needed? Does the person agree or disagree, and what further steps does he or she recommend?

Getting feedback helps you avoid working in a vacuum. It also eases unnecessary fears, builds confidence, and gives you new direction.

POOR SOCIAL SKILLS

The addictive lifestyle isolates the alcoholic or addict from nonaddicted persons, including family, friends, and co-workers. Alcoholics or addicts socialize almost exclusively with other alcoholics or addicts. They think nondrinkers or nonusers are boring losers who never have fun. To alcoholics or addicts, "fun" often means drinking or drugging until they pass out. If others don't want to play their way, they shun them.

Many of the positive events in their life surround alcohol or drugs.[5] Those positive events, and the social nature of drug and alcohol abuse, reinforce abusing behaviors. Alcohol or other drug use forms the basis of their social life.

Even the few friendships they maintain are usually superficial and unsatisfying. Would a real friend knock you unconscious to get your drugs? Would a real friend try to pick up your drunken girlfriend? Would a real friend steal the drugs you hid in your locker for him- or herself? Of course not. Yet these behaviors identify the "friends" of many practicing alcoholics and addicts.

These superficial relationships lead to isolation. At work, practicing alcoholics or addicts often withdraw behind a hostile shell. During times of stress, they lack the human support they need and turn for comfort to their addictive substance, further isolating themselves.[6] Finally, they have no one to talk to, no one who cares, no one who will help.

In recovery, they lose their best friend — alcohol or other drugs. Without the bond of addiction, they then lose their remaining drinking and using friends. They become "socially unacceptable" among practicing alcoholics and drug addicts. They feel uncomfortable and unwanted in their old hangouts. Some, struggling to belong again, relapse into old behaviors. As an old AA adage says, "If you don't want to slip, stay out of slippery places."

You now need to develop new friends and social patterns. You need to learn how to spend your free time without drinking or using and to carry on a conversation without a "relaxer." You need to feel accepted, part of a social group in which you feel comfortable. How can you fulfill these needs?

1. Join a Support Group

Many recovering people find friendship and acceptance within Alcoholics Anonymous, Narcotics Anonymous, or other support groups. In group meetings, you learn and practice new social skills in a safe, loving environment. By listening to and watching other members, you learn acceptable ways to express anger and affection. You learn healthy ways to improve relationships, and you practice saying and doing things that promote your recovery. These practices can help smooth out on-the-job problems that may carry over from using days. Without this support group base, you must build a new social network by yourself.[7]

Group support has been proven the most effective barrier to relapse. Yet some choose another way. A few recovering alcoholics and addicts find their support in church. They often begin their recovery in a support group, then move into a compatible church fellowship. Many combine both support group and church membership, realizing that each performs a different function. Others rely on their family and friends for support and still others rely on no one but themselves.

The last two methods (family and friends, or on your own) put the burden of recovery on those least equipped to bear it. Family and friends are probably exhausted from the strain of your illness and need their own chance to recover. Certainly, they can give you feedback on your behavior and encourage you to get the help you need. But they are not counselors and should not be used as such. As for relying on your own strength, willpower, and knowledge, you are asking a sick person to guide your recovery. With group support, however, dozens of recovering persons help keep you going in the right direction.

Perhaps you tried a support group once, but did not like it. Or you are convinced that your inner resources can meet any threat to your sobriety. Yet, research and experience show that any stressful event can lead back to addictive behavior *if support is not available.*[8] Unsupported abstention, or "white-knuckle sobriety," can lock you into a state of rage, depression, or self-pity that makes you — and those around you — miserable.[9]

Feeling comfortable in a support group usually takes attending at least twenty to thirty meetings, making an effort to meet members, listening to others, getting involved in group activities, and following directions. Weekly attendance helps you make steady progress. Whether or not you socialize with group members after meetings does not matter. You can still learn important social skills.

2. Find New Ways to Spend Your Time

Now that you are in recovery, what will you do with your time? How will you fill those hours that once passed so quickly and now seem so long?

Here are some ways to replace old, destructive behavior with positive behavior.

- What did you enjoy doing when you were clean and sober? Do more of it. If you enjoyed sports, bridge, walking, reading, playing computer games, working in your yard, singing, taking classes, or going to movies, do that more.
- Find something you like to do that includes other people. It should be fun and make you feel good, without involving alcohol or other drugs. Join a ski club, a writers' group, a businessperson's charitable organization, a concert choir, or a bowling team. Go to AA meetings and church functions; sit next to someone and *participate.*
- Emulate a hero. Find someone you admire and do what he or she does that you find interesting or exciting. If you admire your boss and he spends weekends fishing with his children, spend weekends fishing with *your* children. If you admire a co-worker because she ranks high in the city's racquetball standings, learn to play racquetball and compete at your own

level. If you look up to someone because he or she has gone back to complete high school or college, sign up for classes. Sharing an interest gives you a way to start a conversation with persons you admire. Who knows? Maybe a new friendship will develop.

- Be open to learning socially appropriate behavior. Perhaps you seldom speak without using four-letter expletives. Perhaps you have difficulty expressing anger without punching the other guy. Perhaps you still have trouble wanting to drink or use when pressured. You may not know how to enjoy clean-and-sober fun at a party or how to eat dinner without cocktails and wine. You may not know how to talk honestly and openly to the opposite sex or how to discuss your career goals with your boss. Make your home more fun, without drinking or using. Get games to play with your children, a VCR to watch upbeat movies, newspapers and magazines to follow current events, and new records and tapes to keep you dancing. Plan activities that are pleasantly time-consuming for your "danger hours." "Danger hours" may be lunchtime, coffee breaks, immediately after work, before dinner, or after the children go to bed — any time that triggers the thought of drinking or using.

Treatment and aftercare, plus group support, teach you new behaviors. You may also benefit from social skills training with a counselor, therapist, or psychologist. Role playing and videotape feedback can help you rehearse social encounters so you feel comfortable in real-life situations. Assertiveness training can also improve your interpersonal skills.[10]

Like all aspects of recovery, improving social skills takes time, but the effort reaps rich rewards. As you get along better with others, many excuses for drinking or using disappear. Loneliness and self-pity fade; self-respect and that priceless sense of belonging return.

LATE HITS

In football, the term *late hit* means to tackle the ball carrier after the play ends. In recovery, it means to get hit with an unexpected "penalty" after recovery begins.

Many recovering people believe that, once they have started recovery, they can get on with life as if nothing ever happened. But somebody will almost always throw you a late hit.

Glenn, a journeyman machinist, walked into his first AA meeting after his third DWI. He started piecing his life back together. His former boss was glad to rehire him when he found out Glenn was clean and sober. Then, after nine months of sobriety, Glenn got a late hit.

Glenn's probation officer was furious because Glenn had not followed her instructions to go into a structured treatment and aftercare program, as well as AA. Now, she wanted the judge to put him in prison for ninety days to "teach him a lesson." Two AA old-timers went to court with Glenn and convinced the judge that Glenn was staying clean and sober, following a daily AA program, meeting with his sponsor, and working full time.

The judge sentenced Glenn to ten days on a work-release program. Although the sentence could have cost Glenn his job, his employer wanted Glenn to stay. Meanwhile, another company offered Glenn a better job with higher pay. He told the company owner about the sentence, and the prospective boss said, "As long as you're clean and sober, I want you here."

Despite the late hit, Glenn got the chance to choose between two good-paying jobs with employers who accepted his recovery. He took the higher-paying job and served his sentence, grateful that the late hit had not cost him more.

Stopping addictive behavior doesn't guarantee immunity from troubles. A late hit can happen anytime in recovery. You might be audited, fired, fined, sued, or jailed for actions that occurred when you were still drinking or using other drugs.

Your recovery depends on your taking responsibility for your actions. If you owe money, pay it. If you must prove to your employer that you can do a good job, prove it. No matter how long it takes or how much it costs you, stand up, take your licks, and do what is right.

Glenn did not want to face his probation officer or ask AA friends to help him talk to the judge. He did not want to be sentenced, and he did not want to tell his boss. But he did all those things to settle with his past. Now he can face life without worrying about what might hit him when he isn't looking.

DISCRIMINATION

Although you may not be fired, put on probation, or relegated to an invisible position, you may be discriminated against in more subtle ways. For example, you may be excluded from lunches with company executives or left off the memo routing list. Colleagues may fail to include you in decision making. By being excluded, you miss information you need to do your job, make decisions, and contribute to the team.

In some companies, being a recovering alcoholic or addict may make others feel uncomfortable around you or unsure of your suitability for advancement. To some, your past behavior may now seem unacceptable. Once they understand the full reality of what you did, they may punish you with poor evaluations, preventing salary increases. Doug, an electrician with a research and development contractor, is still suffering from that kind of discrimination.

Doug's bar was the warehouse where he worked. It stored barrels of ethanol. Doug helped himself to all he wanted until one day, his boss, supervisor, EAP counselor, and group leader confronted him about his drinking behavior.

85

"I wanted to get my life on a better footing," says Doug. "The next day I made amends. Although I had never been to AA, I realized I had to set things straight, and that night I went to my first meeting."

Management and fellow employees thought anyone who drank ethanol was "the lowest of the low." In addition to being excluded from social occasions, Doug was stripped of his responsibilities. His immediate supervisor assigned him to boring, repetitious tasks and took credit for Doug's accomplishments. Then a new job and new supervisor improved Doug's status.

But shortly after changing jobs, his reinvestigation for security clearance came up. "Since I believe in what I'm doing, I told the truth," Doug says. Unfortunately, the Department of Energy (DOE) didn't reward that honesty. The DOE insisted that he make quarterly reports of his activities. Both his group leader and EAP counselor had to write detailed reports of his AA attendance, work attitude, and health status. Raises stopped dead.

"It comes down to this," says Doug. "I don't believe my skills can be rated much below others in the group, but my salary is the third lowest out of eighty persons. It seems my alcoholism was used as an excuse to depress my salary."

What are the best ways to handle discrimination? Arguing, intimidation, pleading, or filing complaints will not work under most circumstances. Letters of protest, going over your boss's head, and union intervention probably will not bring the most satisfactory solution, either. If your company or union follows a formal grievance procedure, and even if a court of law supports your claim, they may only save your job or win your raise; they won't change people's minds or hearts. What will? Here are a few suggestions.

1. Acceptance

Doug handles discrimination with acceptance, prayer, and gratitude. "I have to get along with these people. I pray for them. I'm glad to have a job and lucky to be alive. I accept many things now so gracefully that it surprises me. I see my situation and I accept it."

Focusing on how others mistreat you may destroy your recovery. Says Wayne Wear:

> I question the person who feels galled and resentful when he goes back to work. I question whether that person can recover. He's struggling with his program. People who are serious about getting well don't have time to think about all the things other people are doing or not doing. It's content versus process. Instead of focusing on the content of what others say and do, they need to get into the process of wellness.

2. Self-Examination

Are you *sure* your addiction is hampering you? Can you think of any other reason you have not been promoted or given a salary increase? Perhaps your complaining attitude turns others away, or your gruff commands create hostility. Perhaps you appear ashamed of your disease, so others feel awkward around you. Or perhaps your work falls below standards. You can concentrate on these shortcomings and improve your overall contribution.

Recovering people are not the only ones who encounter discrimination. Physically handicapped persons face skeptical employers every time they look for a job or seek promotion. But their rejection may not have anything to do with their handicap. They may need to take a harder look at their qualifications.

Does your disease offer a convenient excuse? Maybe your work performance is not as good as it could be. Admitting that fact helps you take your attention off the other guy's prejudices and put it on improving your skills.

3. Make a Special Effort

Be pleasant, cooperative, and positive, without being phony or dishonest. Share information with co-workers. Invite someone to join you for coffee. Offer to help someone finish a project. Throw yourself into your work and enjoy it completely; your zest might change your boss's attitude. Even if it doesn't, it might change *your* attitude.

4. Don't Be a Loner

Join the team. Be part of the group. Make friends in other departments. Develop a wide range of contacts. Show interest in what others do. Think in terms of *we*, not *I* (How can *we* land that new account and work together more effectively?).

5. Stick with the Winners

How do successful people think and act? Spend some time with them, perhaps over lunch, and ask for their suggestions. Don't complain about your boss or company policies that adversely affect you. Stay positive. Talk about the company's goals and how you can contribute. Once you know where the company wants to go, you can make suggestions that pull you onto the team.

6. Admit Defeat

Sometimes, no matter how hard you try, your strategies flop. You can accept the situation with humility and grace, as Doug does, or you can move on. Decide whether the differences that separate you from your boss or co-workers are trivial and transitory, or significant and entrenched. If you cannot see a bright future or if present circumstances keep you upset, start looking for another job. You deserve to work where you are accepted, appreciated, and rewarded on the basis of your performance.

Finding a new job may take less time than you think. Says

Susan Silvano, Executive Vice President of Career Management International:

> People in recovery have a better chance in the marketplace than those people who have problems and haven't admitted those problems to themselves. Substance abusers have been talked to, analyzed, and helped every which way. They know themselves, their limitations, their weaknesses and fears. They know how to follow directions. They are my best clients.

A number of laws and recent court decisions protect recovering people from discrimination. For an overview of your legal rights, see Appendix A.

FINANCIAL PROBLEMS

Practicing alcoholics and addicts usually worry about one primary financial problem: how to get enough money to buy alcohol or other drugs. They may have past-due debts, bounced checks, overdue bills, stolen petty cash, squandered paychecks, or unstable family and business finances, but getting drunk or high is their first priority.

Now, in recovery, those past financial indiscretions can turn into present financial terrors. As the fog of withdrawal clears, recovering people begin to realize the horror of foolish mistakes and careless living and, for the first time, face their financial insecurity. Emotional stress walks hand-in-hand with financial insecurity. For many persons, money is the measure of success, independence, the ability to care for oneself, freedom and self-respect. It may symbolize power, aggressiveness, dominance, authority, or skill mastery.[11]

When money worries plague you, you feel less confident, more anxious; less in control, more powerless; less competent, more insecure; less free, more trapped; less loved, more worthless. These feelings chip away at your serenity and endanger your recovery. As you begin to solve your money problems, you gradually regain your self-esteem and self-respect, and you begin to trust yourself and your ability to cope with financial obligations.

Before you can reach this desirable emotional plane, you need to know where you stand. Recovering persons usually find themselves in one of three financial categories:

1. Lost Little or Nothing

You may still hold your job or own your company. You may still retain your status, salary, and benefits. You may still have your car, home, credit cards and bank account, and group health and life insurance. You may owe the insurance co-payment for treatment and owe small debts to friends and co-workers. None of those debts cause you any serious financial strain. Emotionally, you regret the money you squandered, but you feel deep gratitude that you did not lose more.

Except for repaying personal debts and catching up on bills, you have no other financial responsibilities. Your goals are simple: meet your obligations, give yourself time to gain stability, and keep your career going on an upward track.

2. Working, but Deeply in Debt

You may have lost your car, home, boat, or camper, but you can still earn a living. You may have invested in harum-scarum stocks or get-rich-quick schemes, and all you've got left is worthless paper. You face a stack of bills and past-due notices, and you wonder if you can ever pay them all. You may owe an insurance co-payment or the entire cost of treatment. Your savings and your credit are gone. Your outgo outweighs your income.

You know accepting financial responsibility helps strengthen recovery. You want to repay what you owe, but you don't know how to begin.

You can start by contacting each creditor to work out a plan for smaller payments over a longer time. Most creditors would rather receive small payments than no payments. Or consider contacting your local Consumer Credit Counseling Service, a nonprofit organization. The service will intervene with creditors, even with the Internal Revenue Service. It will set up a plan to pay creditors. But this service does not have the force of law behind it. If your creditors decide to harass you, sue you, garnish your wages, or repossess your furniture, you have no legal means to stop them. If you have too much debt, you may need court authority to protect your assets.

You might qualify for a loan to consolidate your debts. Hal, a recovering alcoholic, had a management-level job and a long-time relationship with a local banker. He borrowed enough money to get out of his financial hole, but he needed nine years to pay it back. Hal says:

> It was really galling for me to make those payments for nine years. But the thing I got from it, when I finally paid off that last responsibility, was the most exhilarating feeling I've ever had in my life — that I had finally done it and been responsible. We all have to pay a price for our past transgressions, that's all there is to it. It's part of our recovery to do what we are told to do.

Paying off your debts over several years need not affect your career. Psychologically, you may feel obliged to stay in your present job until you pay your debts. This reluctance may prevent you from moving to a better-paying job or changing to a more satisfying career. Such a stay-put decision is unnecessary. Hal made two major career changes during those nine years. He shifted from owning his own sales organization to supervising a marketing staff to getting his master's degree and becoming a clinical psychologist. During each move, he continued his payments faithfully. No employer knew of his financial situation, nor needed to know.

3. Starting Over

No one is surprised when practicing alcoholics or addicts lose everything, but it comes as a shock when recovering persons face financial collapse. Yet, it happens all the time. Sometimes, their addiction costs them everything they own, down to pocket change. Years of financial irresponsibility finally catch up. Or emotional problems that surfaced during treatment now prevent them from going back to their old work environment.

Losing everything can make anyone feel frightened, angry, and depressed. Yet these feelings need not overwhelm you or threaten your sobriety. Thousands of recovering persons have overcome financial collapse, rebuilt careers, and become even more successful.

Whatever category fits you, you can begin to put yourself back on sound financial footing. Here are some steps others have taken to deal with their obligations and start over.

A. "Assess your present situation calmly," advises New York psychotherapist Linda Barbenol, who frequently writes and speaks on the psychological aspects of money. "Get a clear picture of your income and outgo. Are you eligible for severance pay or unemployment insurance? Do you have savings, cash, or borrowing power? Make a list of all your resources and determine how much you need to get by on."

B. Determine your net worth, the difference between what you own and what you owe. It does not equal your worth as a person. Says financial planner Nancy Willis, "It's important to separate the financial term 'net worth' from the psychological concept of 'worthiness.' Sometimes, people going through financial traumas may feel unworthy and therefore relate their human value to their financial statement." You may need professional help to determine what assets can be turned into cash or income-producing investments.

C. Reduce your living expenses. Can you appease an irate landlord with a partial payment until you land a new job? Can you rent a one-room apartment instead of a four-bedroom house? Do you really need a telephone? Can you sell your car and use public transportation? How about walking to work instead of taking a taxi? Can you carry a lunch to work instead of eating out? Why not temporarily cancel your piano lessons and weekly manicure? Eliminate frills and get down to basics. Take care of your *needs,* and cut out your *wants.*

D. Lower your sights. Which is better: holding out for a new job at your old salary or having no job? According to Robert Meyers, there are recovering persons who cannot pay their rent but refuse to accept a job below their standards. He says:

> I've seen people be very obstinate, which is detrimental to their recovery. If you're a corporate executive, you may have to start over again down the ladder and work your way up.

Linda Barbenol adds:

> Some people may feel that their personal standards are lowered if they take a lower paying job. Think of the situation as a practical decision for the short range. The rent does have to be paid, right? You are taking care of what has to be done. You will gain self-esteem in the process and make money too.

E. Don't set yourself up for failure. Many alcoholics and addicts have unrealistic expectations. If they can't be president of the bank, they don't want a less prestigious job. If they can't sing the lead, they won't accept a minor part. If they can't have the biggest territory, they won't move anywhere smaller. Their dreams and schemes are often unrealistic and grandiose. Because they set unreachable goals, they fail. Failure breeds self-contempt, which breeds more failure.

Recovery means learning to moderate thinking and behavior, to succeed in small steps. Says Meyers, "You try to get minimal successes and build on them to bigger successes. The best way to raise self-esteem is to find something you do well and get some minimal gains. Then you can continue to grow."

F. Keep your emotions out of financial decisions. Says Barbenol, "Often people experiencing negative financial change face so much stress they cannot function. They become paralyzed. Some fast decisions must be made, but don't jump to relieve the pressure. Stress overload causes improper decisions. Use advisors to help you in areas with which you are unfamiliar."

Allow your emotions to settle down. Willis says, "Give yourself some time to deal with the psychological strain. While allowing the spirit to heal, one can move slowly toward long-term plans to cope with practical details."[12]

G. Make short-term and long-term goals. For the short-term, you may need to earn enough money to buy a meal or pay the rent. To do that, you may need to borrow from family or friends, accept a job beneath your ability level, work two or three part-time jobs, or stay in a job that annoys you. Consider these decisions short-term expediencies while you look for long-term solutions. When you realize your present situation will not last forever, you can accept it more easily.

Says counselor Jonathan Hartshorne, "More pain can be tolerated in a short-term plan if you have a long-term plan to back you up. Even in a tough situation, maintain your integrity; protect your sobriety."

Long-term planning should focus on getting you into a working and living situation that enhances recovery. You may need to build up cash in a savings account or money market fund. You may need to improve your credit. You may need education to help you toward a more interesting or better-paying career. You may want to move to an area that offers more opportunities. You can reach these goals if you take careful steps, not unplanned leaps. You want to land on your feet, not fall on your face.

H. Understand your insurance status. "You are going to have insurance difficulties if you are disconnected from the system," says Willis. As long as you stay connected, usually through a large company's group insurance plan, you can get the health and life insurance coverage you need. But, if you become disconnected — lose your job, forget to convert a group plan to individual coverage, fail to pay premiums, or get canceled due to high risk or excessive claims — you will have difficulty in obtaining insurance, except at unusually high rates. (See Appendix B for suggestions on applying for insurance.)

I. Find out the advantages and disadvantages of declaring bankruptcy. (See Appendix C for an overview of the proceedings available and their features.) Many recovering persons face debts that threaten their business, their home, their car, and their way of life. By declaring bankruptcy, they can legally discharge those debts through a liquidation proceeding or restructure debt through a reorganization proceeding. Federal statutes provide the legal means to clear away debt while keeping sufficient funds to meet your living expenses.

Before you say yes or no to bankruptcy, analyze the ramifications. Filing bankruptcy can stay on your credit record for up to ten years. Banks may refuse to grant you a loan, and credit card companies may turn down your application. Nonetheless, reestablishing credit takes less time and effort than it did fifteen years ago. Many local retail firms, for example, extend financing immediately following a bankruptcy.

Even if declaring bankruptcy makes good financial sense and causes barely a ripple in your credit, you may balk for emotional reasons. Many people fear the judgment of friends, family, and business associates. They fear the loss of credit, a crutch they can lean on for pleasures or cash-flow emergencies. They believe bankruptcy will shatter their image and crush their self-esteem. Fear, ego-involvement, and false pride keep them locked in a self-imposed financial prison.

Yet, admitting financial failure can teach a person important lessons:

- How to accept reality and personal limitations.
- How to ask for help.
- How to give compassion and understanding to others.
- How to survive.

Take a small step to find out whether or not bankruptcy would ease your pressures. Read a few books and articles on the subject. Make an appointment with a lawyer to get more information. Talk to others who have declared bankruptcy.

J. Get advice from qualified persons. Don't take financial directions from your sponsor, aftercare group, therapist, minister, or recovering friends without getting all the advice you can from qualified financial counselors. Then give your options careful, prayerful consideration.

❊ ❊ ❊ ❊ ❊

Incredible changes happen in treatment facilities, halfway houses, and support groups. You want to keep those changes alive, keep the effects meaningful in your life. You don't want reality to crush them. At the same time, you must adjust from the treatment culture to the real world. And, as every recovering person knows, the rules are different.

Says Hartshorne, "It's important not to compromise yourself. You want to bring the skills you learned in the treatment center to the workplace, not lapse into old ways of behaving. You want to keep on integrating that new behavior."

To keep that process happening, it's helpful to remember these three guidelines:

First, take aftercare and continuing support seriously. Without them, your recovery will stall. In individual and group sessions, you can talk about problems and issues, discover feelings underlying your reactions, discuss strategies and tactics that might apply, and experiment with potential responses. These practice sessions increase your adaptability and squelch the power of relapse-provoking events. They also build fellowship, a sense of belonging, social skills, self-esteem, faith in yourself, and faith in a Higher Power.

Second, begin making lifestyle changes immediately. Don't postpone them until you feel more comfortable, more rested. After treatment, you feel exhausted — inspired, uplifted, hope-filled, but emotionally drained. You want time to catch your breath and regain energy. You plan to make changes, but later, when you feel stronger. Don't wait for later. Don't postpone taking steps that might save your sanity, your recovery, and your life. Says Hartshorne, "The danger in postponing lifestyle changes is in letting things slide until inertia and self-compromise set in."

Third, work your recovery program. Do what you are told. If your counselor tells you to write a letter to your long-dead father, write it. If your sponsor tells you to get down on your knees morning and evening, get down there. If your therapist tells you to read page 449 of *Alcoholics Anonymous,* read it. Even if you don't understand and don't agree, do it anyway. You are taking a long, arduous journey through dangerous territory, and you don't know the route. Others have been there and can lead the way. Let them help you keep on keeping on.

ENDNOTES
Chapter Four

1. *Alcoholics Anonymous* 3rd ed. (New York: Alcoholics Anonymous World Services, Inc., 1976), 164.

2. Andrew S. Grove, *One-on-One with Andy Grove* (New York: Penguin Books, 1988), 133-134.

3. Anne Wilson Schaef and Diane Fassel, *The Addictive Organization* (San Francisco: Harper & Row, 1988), 143.

4. Grove, *One-on-One,* 135.

5. Sister Bea, address to the National Alcoholics Anonymous Women's Conference, 14 February 1987, Albuquerque, New Mexico.

6. Deborah L. Rhoads, "A Longitudinal Study of Life Stress and Social Support Among Drug Abusers," *International Journal of the Addictions* 16 (1981): 205.

7. Ibid., 206.

8. Ibid., 206.

9. Richard B. Seymour and David E. Smith, *Drugfree* (New York: Facts On File Publications, 1987), 6-7.

10. W. L. Ferrel and J. P. Galassi, "Assertion Training and Human Relations Training in the Treatment of Chronic Alcoholics," *International Journal of the Addictions* 16 (1981): 959.

11. Bonnie Siverd, *Count Your Change* (New York: Priam Books, Arbor House, 1983), 15.

12. Nancy K. Willis, "Solving the Financial Crises of Life's Upheavals," *Business Outlook* (20 October 1986): 8.

CHAPTER FIVE

FINDING THE RIGHT PLACE FOR RECOVERY

You cannot get well in a sick environment. Every organization or workplace has an environment that either fosters your recovery or undermines it. An unhealthy work environment can trigger addictive patterns that may lead to relapse, even after years of sobriety. Addictive patterns of interaction and behavior can exist within individuals, groups, teams, departments, companies, organizations, industries, and entire professions. Addiction has been described as an organizational disease. Two organizational consultants, Anne Wilson Schaef and Diane Fassel, describe an organization as addictive in this way:

> Many of our organizations are addictive organizations embedded in an addictive society. By this we mean that many organizations are affected by addictions and an addictive workview and even themselves function exactly like an active individual addict.[1]

Since your recovery comes first, you need to ask yourself one vital question:

CAN I RECOVER HERE?

It is a hard question to answer honestly. You will probably want to say yes because you feel safe in a known environment, even if it is a sick environment. If you say no, you must decide to change. That risk is likely to provoke fear and self-doubt. You may feel much safer and more confident if you stay where you are and shut the door on the inner voice that says, *I cannot recover here.* When you shut that door, you compromise yourself. An honest look at your work environment will give you a giant step toward wellness.

The signs of sickness or health you should look for are the same signs that were evident in your addiction. Remember how you felt and acted when you were drinking or using other drugs? Sick environments show the same symptoms. Here is a partial list that shows the differences between sick and healthy attitudes and behavior tendencies.

Sick/Addictive	*Healthy/Recovering*
Denial of problems	Acceptance of problem, humility
Lying, dishonesty, gossip, secrecy	Honesty, openness, straight talk
Power driven, obsessed with winning	Shared mutual goals, participation
Crisis oriented	Planning with flexibility, realistic deadlines
Perfectionism, unrealistic standards and goals	Reachable goals and challenges
Materialistic	Spiritually based
Ethical breakdown	Ethical practices
Blaming others	Taking responsibility

Sick/Addictive	*Healthy/Recovering*
Manipulating	Helping others
Self-protectiveness	Expressing feelings
Covering up mistakes	Acknowledging mistakes
Poor working relationships	Respecting self and others
Need to impress others	Internalizing values

Now ask yourself: *What symptoms do I observe in my work environment? Are they mostly sick/addictive or healthy/recovering?* If you label your work environment as sick/addictive, you must face this uncomfortable fact: *Recovery in a sick environment would be very difficult.*

Let me add three "if" qualifiers. You can recover in a sick environment:

1. *If you can separate yourself — mentally, emotionally, and physically, if necessary — from the people, events, product, goals, and management style, that exist around you.* Rarely does this kind of detachment lead to business success, and it certainly isn't conducive to fun, pleasure, or enjoyment in your career.

2. *If you can share your feelings honestly with someone close to you within the organization.* Someone else becomes a sounding board for your perceptions and helps prevent you from getting drawn into the prevailing craziness.

3. *If a genuine recovery process is going on inside the organization.* Many organizations are trying to shift from a sick/addictive system to a healthy/recovering system. If this shift takes place — not just as a temporary expediency to quell dissatisfaction within the ranks — it probably will bring about changes that promote your recovery. It might be worth hanging in there.

101

TYPES OF WORK ENVIRONMENTS

When you evaluate your prospects for recovery at work, consider four elements that comprise your work environment:

- your overall profession,
- your specific job,
- your supervisors and co-workers, and
- the organization or workplace.

Each can be characterized according to the impact it has on your recovery.

Hostile Environment

The hostile work environment creates extreme anxiety. Supervisors may put constant pressure on recovering persons, watching them, hoping to catch a small error, waiting for a reason to take punitive action. Managers may purposely misunderstand what the recovering person says and does, and they may refuse to acknowledge or reward performance improvement.

The boss, co-workers, or customers may reject recovery values, such as honesty, openness, shared feelings, and accepting the consequences of one's actions. Instead, they blame their problems and failures on the recovering person's "poor attitude." They refuse to discuss misunderstandings, preferring to write vague memos or delegating a third person to deliver a message. Administrators may ridicule or condemn the recovering person's disease, as in this revealing scene:

Ed Furtado, Employee Assistance Administrator for a large utility company, remembers a woman administrator who attended the 1987 White House Conference on Drug Addiction. The woman represented a company of over one hundred employees.

During a discussion about the merits of EAPs, she burst out with this tirade: "I'm getting uptight about helping these drunks. My son died of alcoholism, which is a disease of choice. Why do I have to pay all these taxes to help people who have choices? Why do I have to start an Employee Assistance Program? It's not fair that I'm rewarding that drunk or drug addict with time off with pay, when I've got other people that don't get time off and don't need special attention!"

Her outburst reveals the judgmental, righteous attitude typical of a hostile work environment.

The hostile work environment actively rejects the recovering person's ideas, performance, participation, values, and rights. It treats the recovering person as a direct threat to its existence.

What to do? Leave. Bobby Sykes, Ph.D., recommends:

> Try to maintain an appropriate level of functioning until you can get out. It's not healthy in the long run to always be under that kind of pressure. Even for the non-addict, it's too much pressure to live with on a daily basis. Begin to research ways to change your employment.

An Enabling Environment

This work environment can kill you with kindness. Rather than being impatient and punitive, it goes too far in the other direction. Supervisors give too much time and sympathy to recovering staff or look the other way when they see warning signs of relapse. Management may fail to enforce the company's EAP policy because "good old Joe" is a valued employee. They let him get away with missing AA meetings or skipping a weekly counseling session "just this once." Co-workers avoid talking about the recovering person's experience and pretend nothing happened. Everyone makes excuses for the recovering person's mistakes, forgives inappropriate outbursts, takes over some of his or her responsibilities, and lowers performance standards for that person's job.

People in the enabling work environment show many symptoms of codependency, such as taking care of people who are perfectly able to take care of themselves, covering up and making excuses for them, denying reality, and taking on their failures and problems. By treating the recovering person like a sick child, these people foster a self-pitying, "poor me" attitude that can lead the recovering person to relapse.

Can you recover in an enabling work environment? Probably not. Susan Silvano gives this example of what can happen:

> I had a client recently who had been through treatment three times. Every time he fell off the wagon, the company gave him another chance. I told the company, "This is ridiculous. The company is enabling. If we don't think he's curable, we recommend firing him. And the company needs to reevaluate its policies toward substance abuse and treatment."
>
> Finally, the client accepted responsibility for his own actions. He did recover, but because of the enabling environment, we recommended that he not stay there. He had a long history of problems with that company, and we felt he would continue to have problems there. He got a new position in about three weeks and is very successful.
>
> It's mercy versus justice. We want to be merciful, but justice works better with recovering people. There are just enough hugs and kisses, and you have to stop that after a while.

You might meet with your team or closest co-workers and discuss enabling or codependent behaviors. Ask your EAP, treatment, or aftercare counselor to join the session. Together, you can help them recognize that what they are doing is destructive to you, them, and the organization. You might suggest a written contract that details what enabling behaviors will not be tolerated.

You might select one or two co-workers who support your recovery, believe in straight talk, and do not play enabling roles.

They can become your reality testers. Let them know how you need to be treated. Ask them to warn you when you allow enablers to manipulate you. Talk to them frequently about your work relationships and ask for feedback.

You must confront co-workers at the time they attempt to enable, tell them what they are doing wrong, and let them know how to correct it. Say something like this: "Mary, I don't want you to make excuses for me. I need to be responsible for my mistakes. You'd help me more by treating me like everyone else." Keep saying the same thing to the same person. Your firmness and consistency may bring changes.

These efforts can make your worklife honest, open, responsible, caring, productive, and fun. You can become a role model. But the burden of modeling behavior can weigh heavily on your shoulders, especially if you are new to recovery. Sometimes you need all your energy to stay clean and sober and to attend support group meetings. You do not have the strength to educate, confront, or guide anyone. Besides, those enabling behaviors may feel very comforting when you return from treatment. You may not want to change them right away, even if new behaviors are what you need most.

The enabling environment can comfort and pamper, but it makes the recovering person feel needy, dependent, and inadequate. With enough time in recovery (plus enough clout within the organization to call the shots), you can prevent being swallowed whole. You can establish your guidelines for the behavior you will accept from others. Then, if you can't change them, leave them.

An Impersonal Environment

This work environment can bring on low-level depression. You are tolerated, but not accepted; you are allowed to stay as long as you meet performance standards; you are essentially alone as you deal with stress and problems.

The impersonal work environment drives you to depression because it increases your loneliness and isolation. Things go on that you know nothing about. Secrets, closed doors, and misinformation keep you confused, lacking information you need to do a quality job.

The impersonal work environment may ignore ethics and honesty, then respond to your protests as though you were a traitor. Friendships seldom develop and deep sharing never happens. The lack of compassion and closeness generates apprehension. You dread going to work because it is not a positive, healthy place.

Communication is more likely to take place, not through intimate conversations or participative meetings, but in stilted memos, unnecessary forms, and company-wide announcements. As long as you follow rules and comply with your supervisor's instructions, you fit in. When work becomes impersonal, it can kill enthusiasm, energy, friendship, warmth, self-respect, and growth. To the recovering person, this work environment may feel like death.

Can you recover in an impersonal work environment? Possibly. Much depends on your personality, the type of work you do, and your outside support system. If you have an introverted personality, you may adapt well where you can keep to yourself, where others do not poke into your personal affairs, where you can deal with problems your own way. On the other hand, this environment could drive you so deeply inside yourself that you become paranoid or antisocial. For extroverts, it could cause extreme frustration, hostility, and resentment.

If the type of work you do requires an isolated setting (a research laboratory, library, or studio, for example), you may feel comfortable in an impersonal environment. A lot of personal interaction might distract and dismay you. If your work puts you in life-threatening or heart-wrenching situations, or if you are, for example, a police officer or hospital emergency room medic, an impersonal work environment might help protect your emotional balance. But an important part of your recovery is learning to recognize and deal with your feelings, not covering them under layers of stilted official procedures.

Your outside support system can save your job, your sanity, and your recovery. It lets you talk to people who know you, love you, understand you, and want the best for you. The people in your outside support system — your aftercare counselor, EAP contact, therapist, recovering friends, supportive family members, minister or rabbi, support group, and sponsor — help you live a human and spiritual existence. They help you remember who you are, what you are, where you are going, and what you must do to get there. They may give you the only smile you see all day, but that one human contact can pull you through.

A Supportive Environment

The supportive work environment fosters interaction. It creates a system in which people support one another. It builds teamwork and participation as it respects the feelings, rights, and values of the individual. It establishes an atmosphere of compassion and tolerance in which mistakes can happen and problems can be solved.

This environment is noncompetitive. It doesn't pit employees against each other to battle for promotions, bonuses, salary increases, awards, or recognition. It nurtures individual creativity and achievement by providing a forum where ideas can be openly expressed. Because employees don't compete, they can freely share their knowledge and insights with others. They feel less suspicious, less guarded, and less anxious. Consequently, they feel more psychologically and physically healthy.[2]

This noncompetitive, team approach thrives because the organizational structure allows less segmentation. Executive, staff, and line management's responsibilities frequently merge; supervisors seek problem-solving input from department personnel; employees from the mail room and assembly line contribute ideas for improving quality and productivity. Often, top management establishes an "open door" or "shirtsleeve" policy that stimulates informal communication. Employees can say, "We've got a problem," and talk it over person to person.

The company practices the theme, "A happy, healthy employee is a productive employee, and productive employees are good for business." An Employee Assistance Program helps employees find assistance for marriage, family, financial, and career problems, as well as for health and educational needs. Exercise facilities, team sports, and family get-togethers offer relaxation and fun. A professional development program encourages employees to learn, grow, and advance. Industry networking brings outside information into the organization, bringing in a refreshing flow of stimulating ideas. This "happy, healthy" theme discourages compulsive work habits and codependency and encourages responsible, balanced living.

The company ethically produces a quality product. Employees take pride in their work and their company, and employees believe in their product. Most employees would not change jobs if you paid them twice as much. Recovering employees will not budge.

Do organizations like this actually exist, or do they live only in employees' dreams? They exist. In some organizations, they exist within only a department or division, a branch office, or a field location. In others, the entire organization is shifting from a sick/addictive system to a healthy/recovering system. When you find these bright lights of wellness, you have found the right place for recovery.

IS YOUR JOB A DANGER ZONE?

You may work for the greatest organization on earth, but still encounter elements that could lead to relapse. Here is a quiz to help you evaluate how your current job affects your recovery.

Circle Yes or No.

1. Is your salary adequate to meet your needs? (Yes) No
2. Does your salary reflect your ability and contribution? (Yes) No
3. Is your daily routine interesting? (Yes) No
4. Does your work offer a frequent change of pace? (Yes) No
5. Does management set reachable goals, quotas, and schedules? Yes (No)
6. Do you have the necessary equipment to do your job? (Yes) No
7. Are you physically safe? (Yes) No
8. Is planning adequate to prevent frequent crises? Yes (No)
9. Does the organization exist for socially valuable goals? Yes No
10. Do supervisors include you in goal setting, decision making, or change implementation? (Yes) No
11. Are responsibilities delegated? (Yes) No
12. Do you work at or above your level of skill, education, and experience? (Yes) No
13. Can you talk freely to superiors? (Yes) No
14. Are your ideas and opinions considered important? (Yes) No
15. Can you handle the daily pressures? (Yes) No
16. Are your co-workers skilled and experienced enough to do their share? Yes No
17. Does your spouse and family approve of and admire your job? (Yes) No
18. Do you receive recognition for your contributions? (Yes) No
19. Is your job description clear? (Yes) No

20. Can you move up the organizational ladder?   (Yes) No
21. Do you understand on what basis your performance is evaluated?   (Yes) No
22. Is fun, laughter, joking part of your work environment?   (Yes) No
23. Do you admire your supervisor?   Yes No
24. Is your type of job secure?   (Yes) No
25. Do you feel accepted and supported?   Yes No

This test is the author's original, unvalidated, unscientific adaptation of concepts from the works of Anne Wilson Schaef, Terence Gorski, and Robert Dato.

"Yes" answers indicate those elements that are positive, healthy, and recovery-oriented. "No" answers indicate problem areas that lead to fear, anxiety, frustration, insecurity, resentment, lack of motivation, and boredom.

WHAT NEEDS TO BE CHANGED?

First, what *not* to change. Don't change your values. Now that you are making progress in recovery, you are getting in touch with the things that mean the most to you. When you compromise your values, you compromise your recovery. Your job, career, and work environment should be aligned with both your personal and recovery values, not in conflict with them.

Don't change your recovery program. Some recovering people need to attend a support group meeting every day. That daily contact keeps them from slipping back into old thinking patterns and behavior. It helps them learn healthier ways to deal with pressure. Others make progress with fewer meetings, but need time with a counselor, therapist, or sponsor. Those who are working on a Step in their Twelve Step program need to continue that effort. You may need to rearrange your work or travel schedule to accommodate a program meeting or set aside time during a busy day for reading, writing, prayer, meditation, or a telephone call to a recovering friend. Don't eliminate the program "medicine" that is healing you.

Don't change everything at once. Many recovering persons panic and bolt. They run away from their job or their career. They think they are protecting their sobriety, but in fact, they are running from circumstances they need to confront. They might give their recovery more strength and integrity if they stayed in their old job and experimented with new behaviors. If you hang in and hold on, you might get a chance to learn the lessons you need to learn. If you leave prematurely, you will be forced to learn those lessons at the next place or the next.

One lesson you may learn is that your career or profession doesn't fit you. An honest look may show you do not enjoy your work, and that it doesn't match your values. If so, you may need to change. Discovering where you belong in the work world is a process of self-discovery that builds self-confidence and enhances recovery.

Another lesson is learning whether you can handle the functions and pressures of your present job. You look at

- the goals of the organization,
- your tasks,
- the quality of supervision,
- management expectations,
- the pace of production,
- the degree of emotional involvement,
- the time commitment, and
- the physical energy required.

If you can handle or reduce the stressors, you will not need to change jobs. If you cannot do either, you must look for a job that matches your personality, your values, your strengths and weaknesses, and your recovery needs.

For example, if you are trying to deal with stress management or anger management, you may not be able to handle a job in the stock market. If you feel uncomfortable and uneasy making decisions, you may need to step down from a leadership position. If you worry about financial insecurity, you might give up your free-lance or consulting position for a steady, salaried job, at least temporarily. As you discover what you can handle, you will make choices that move you closer to a working situation that is compatible with your recovery.

Perhaps the only changes that need to be made involve work life skills. Often, newly recovering people face massive unfinished business. Rather than a career change or job switch, they must undertake extensive repair work. Relationships need to be mended, responsibilities need to be understood and accepted, and trust needs to be built — all of which take time and might best be done by staying put.

NINE JOB-REPAIRING STRATEGIES

Your addiction may have shattered relationships with supervisors, co-workers, clients, and industry associates. You can try one or more of these nine job-repairing strategies to overcome the past.

1. Admission of Guilt

If you have done something dishonest, irresponsible, insulting, or harmful, you can expose it to the light of truth and remove its power. You will find great relief in admitting it.

A heart-to-heart talk with each person involved may let you start over with a clean slate. You should find a quiet time and a private place where both you and the other person can talk.

You don't need to go into a long, guilty explanation; a simple "this is what happened" will do. You might add that you have changed your life so this kind of incident will not reoccur. This reassurance will help put the past to rest. But don't waste the other person's time and patience by merely trying to get back in his or her good graces. Changing your behavior in recovery will heal more than promises or apologies.

Not all such scenes end with a friendly handshake. Some people may not accept your apology. They may feel angry or refuse to work with you. All you can do is accept their decision with as much dignity as possible. At least you have disclosed the incident and can stop being afraid someone will find out. This admission goes a long way toward releasing guilt and shame and finding self-respect.

2. Restitution

Once you admit a mistake or wrongdoing, you will gain a large measure of self-respect by offering to make restitution, even if repayment would be a hardship. If the other person accepts, the two of you can work out a mutually agreeable plan. Your determination to be responsible for your past actions may gain respect, even if it is grudgingly given.

Making restitution — what Step Nine of AA's Twelve Steps calls "amends" — is a centuries-old way to release your guilt and return yourself to a trustworthy status. Step Nine warns, however, that amends should not be made if doing so would harm another person. If your admission would incriminate someone else or make innocent persons suffer for your mistakes, you must make restitution anonymously or not at all. Your counselor, minister, or Twelve Step sponsor can help you decide the best way to handle this conflict.

3. Reassurance of Career Commitment

Your boss and co-workers want to know that you will put your best efforts into achieving shared goals. You can show them, by your attitude and actions, that your old behavior no longer threatens them. You are a new person, and this new person acts honorably, honestly, and responsibly. Your promptness, consideration, effort, and participation will give them evidence of your new resolve.

Let what you say to those around you reflect your new attitude. A remark like, "I'm really getting excited about this project," or "Wouldn't it be great if we landed this contract!" shows that you care about your job and the company's goals. Your enthusiasm reassures everyone that you are giving a 100 percent effort.

4. Setting New Goals

How long has it been since you had a performance review? How long since reevaluating your career goals? As a chemically dependent person, you may have slid by your once-a-year review with a few insincere promises and unreachable goals. Now it is time to set new career goals and discuss your goals with your supervisor.

While you may want to set impressive new goals, your best approach is to start small, with modest, short-term goals. Instead of a goal like "reorganize the whole shipping department," you might try for "clean out the storage room" and "set up an intercom system." These specific goals help focus your efforts and give you little successes on which to build.

When you determine your goals, you can discuss them with your supervisor, as well as discussing the direction you want to take. He or she will want to know what progress or setbacks you encounter and when you reach the goal. With one goal behind you, you can set another.

Taking small steps makes large projects seem less intimidating. In addition, each success builds your self-confidence and assures your supervisor that you are committed to making changes. Once you prove that you can achieve short-term goals, you can work closely with your supervisor to establish long-term goals that increase your contribution to the company and boost your chances for promotion.

5. Depersonalizing the Situation

Recovering alcoholics and addicts are not the only ones with feelings. Other people can feel hurt, angry, or resentful too. Sometimes emotions crackle so loudly through a conversation that you cannot hear or convey a clear message. When feelings dominate a work relationship, nobody can perform effectively.

You can depersonalize the situation by talking in terms of performance goals and objectives, stressing what needs to be done and what steps need to be taken.

If your past behavior stands in the way of open communication, your apology may remove that block. That act lets the other person know that you respect his or her feelings and you want to get on with present business. When you ask outright whether that person can forget personalities and concentrate on objectives, you shift away from finding a villain to solving the problem at hand.

6. Improving Productivity

Few things repair a job situation as effectively as outstanding performance. Management may be leery about your commitment and goals. But when you perform steadily over many months and you bump up your productivity, managers become believers.

One-shot deals will not impress them. Landing a new account, selling a large order, or finishing a major project isn't likely to convince them that you are a changed person. You could probably do those things when you were drinking or using. But could you do them steadily, regularly, or reliably over a long time period? Now you can. Your persistence reinforces your commitment and impresses even the skeptical.

7. Asking for Direction

Recovering people often don't want help, and they may seldom ask for instructions. When something goes wrong, they may cover it up and make matters even worse. If they become belligerent when someone offers a suggestion or corrects an error, they can make a lot of mistakes — and enemies.

If you recognize your limitations, you can look to others for direction. Going to your boss for help can mean a shortcut to a solution. He or she probably has more power and experience to make the decisions that will remedy a problem or break a stalemate. You may think asking for directions makes you appear weak and indecisive; on the contrary, if you handle it well, you will appear a practical problem-solver.

The trick to asking for directions is to already know the best options. When you approach your boss for instructions, you can offer choices and solutions, and let the boss decide which course looks best. He or she usually wants to hear the facts clearly, without embellishment or emotionalism. Making excuses or blaming others only makes you seem defensive and childish. Taking responsibility, accepting the boss's decision, and carrying it out efficiently will help in gaining both self-respect and the respect of your boss.

Caution: Whatever you do, don't *assume* you know what the boss will do or decide. (In fact, never assume you know what *anybody* will do or decide.) Making an excuse like "I assumed you'd okay the order" or "I thought you'd disapprove any overtime" annoys your superior. Checking first saves you from making embarrassing excuses.

8. Urging More Frequent Feedback and Evaluation

Those once-a-year evaluations can make a person feel paranoid. Such waiting and worrying is dangerous for recovering persons, and unnecessary. A weekly meeting with your supervisor will cut down suspicions and build up confidence.

You might ask your boss to set aside ten minutes once a week to discuss your performance. A quick get-together makes sure both of you are going in the same direction. He or she may offer suggestions or comments that help improve your contribution. If so, be sure to take notes and confirm any agreements in a brief memo. You can use that memo as a checklist for your next meeting. Here is what one recovering alcoholic did when she was on the verge of losing her job.

> Terri, a bubbly secretary, was promoted to administrative assistant to an ambitious commercial real estate broker. Her friendly, outgoing personality immediately irritated her all-business boss. Terri treated him like a friend, not a boss, and thought her position with the company was so secure that she could take long phone calls from her AA friends and leave work early to go to meetings. She was crushed when the office manager told

116

Terri that the broker would fire her unless her behavior changed radically.

Terri's AA sponsor suggested a businesslike talk to reassure her boss of her career commitment and to ask for direction. Terri asked her boss to tell her when he spotted a problem and to schedule a Friday afternoon evaluation session during the following four weeks. Terri wrote an informal memo that outlined the agreed-upon behaviors she would try to implement, and she asked her boss to sign it. She used that document as the basis for their Friday talks.

Six weeks later, Terri's supervisor congratulated her for having won the wholehearted approval of her boss. However, Terri believes she needs a work environment that is warmer, more personal, and more fun. While she looks for a new job, she knows that her present position is secure.

9. Submitting to Company Guidelines

You cannot expect to repair on-the-job relationships unless you comply willingly with company guidelines and restrictions. You might be required to attend AA meetings as part of your EAP contract, or to meet with your counselor or therapist regularly. Often, the company will prohibit a recovering person from working around restricted equipment or traveling where counseling or group support is not available.

Eventually, when your probationary period ends and your employer's confidence returns, you can enjoy the full rights and privileges of your job. Meanwhile, if you show willingness to follow the rules, you will go a long way toward rebuilding your status.

❀ ❀ ❀ ❀ ❀

Some jobs cannot be saved, some relationships cannot be healed — not because of *you*, but because of *them*. The workplace and the people in it may be too sick to forgive, to accept, to befriend, or to support. If you have tried these job-repairing strategies, but your boss still seems lukewarm and your co-workers still avoid you, you have no choice but to consider moving on. You can endure feeling like an outcast if you know it will end. But you cannot recover in an atmosphere of suspicion and distrust, nor can you do your job effectively with half-hearted cooperation. Pack it up and move it somewhere else. The stress and disruption of making a job or career change is preferable to jeopardizing your sobriety when your life is at stake.

ENDNOTES
Chapter Five

1. Anne Wilson Schaef and Diane Fassel, *The Addictive Organization* (San Francisco: Harper & Row, 1988), 4.

2. Ibid., 17.

CHAPTER SIX

THE CLEAN-AND-SOBER JOB HUNT

If your present job is hindering your recovery, you don't have to feel trapped. You have choices. If you let go of a harmful situation, you can create a new setting that nurtures your recovery. Ideally, you will match your inner strengths, personality, interests, values, and recovery goals to the appropriate job. Then you can concentrate on finding the workplace in which your recovery can flourish.

This process begins with *you*. You have to look honestly at who you are and what works best for you. You have to analyze your recovery and determine what hurts or helps it. Then you can establish guidelines to evaluate future career opportunities. With your own set of career guidelines, you will be less likely to rush into another job situation that brings up the same, harmful problems. You can evaluate equally interesting offers and choose the one that best fits your needs.

Some career counselors suggest you make lists of what (not *who*) you like and dislike in your present job. What responsibilities do you enjoy? What actions make you feel competent and satisfied? What duties do you avoid, put off, or fail to do at all? Ideally, you want a job that allows you to do more of the functions you like and fewer of those you dislike.

Other career counselors administer tests to spot hidden talents and interests. These techniques help you explore career directions that would tap your inner resources and bring you more success and satisfaction. Such testing takes time, money, and perceptive interpretation. If you cannot afford the fees charged by private career counselors, you can usually get similar services through a local college or university placement office.

Another effective approach is one developed by Jerry L. Fletcher, Ed. D., president and founder of High Performance Dynamics, Inc., a California management consulting firm that teaches companies and individuals to achieve sustained high performance. Dr. Fletcher suggests you list job factors that bring out your best. Whenever these factors exist, you become interested and motivated. Invariably, you end up with a successful conclusion. Without those factors, you become bored, restless; you have to force yourself to perform even minimally.

By looking back over past successes, you can isolate those factors that, when present, keep you happily producing at your peak. As you consider three or more past successes, ask yourself such questions as these:

1. What initially interested you about each job or assignment? What made it seem challenging?

2. How did you relate to others who were working on the same assignment? What kind of relationships helped you produce your best work? (Examples: "They left me alone to work." Or, "We had a close, highly interactive working relationship." Or, "There was one person who helped me bounce around ideas.")

3. What responsibilities did you want and what ones did you gladly relinquish to others?

4. How much time were you willing to give to each project? Did you work on only one thing at a time, or did you prefer to work on several projects at once?

5. How much effort did you expend? In a short burst of energy, or steadily over a period of time?

6. How did you bring the assignment or project to an end?

7. What rewards made each project seem worthwhile?[1]

After analyzing your answers, you might discover such factors as these:

1. I am most effective when I originate an idea or get it from the company president.

2. I prefer to work alone and report directly to the person in charge.

3. I work best when I am responsible for original concept, client contact, proposal, and presentation; I can leave details and follow-up to others.

4. I can stay interested in the same project for about three months, then I need to finish it and start another. I dislike long, theoretical, never-ending assignments.

5. I work best on projects that have a potentially big impact on the company. Because it seems important, I put a great deal of effort into it for a short period of time.

6. I like a dramatic conclusion to a project, such as an awards banquet, grand opening, or press conference.

7. I need the personal recognition of the company president and top executives.

These insights pinpoint job factors that spark your interest and keep you highly motivated. You can use these factors as criteria to evaluate your present job or to negotiate terms when one is offered.

Next, you might list the factors you need to keep your recovery progressing. These should include such items as (1) how much time you need for reading, meditation, prayer, counseling, or support group attendance; (2) when you regularly see your counselor, therapist, or sponsor; (3) how often you need to talk to other recovering persons; (4) what health/fitness plan you need to follow; (5) what stressors you want to eliminate; and (6) what work environment you need.

Your list might look something like this:

1. I need thirty minutes a day for reading, meditation, and prayer. I attend an evening aftercare session and three NA meetings a week.

2. I see my sponsor every other week, preferably on Friday afternoons or Saturday mornings.

3. I like to have lunch with recovering friends at least once a week, but I seldom need to telephone someone during working hours.

4. My doctor recommends a forty-five-minute walk, three times a week. I need a well-rounded meal, not junk food, and prefer to eat at an inexpensive cafeteria.

5. I want to eliminate working with people who are using drugs. I want to stop taking work home on weekends.

6. I like an upbeat, happy work environment with plenty of people around me. I would prefer that my boss know about my recovery and understand my program.

With these kinds of lists, you have *guidelines* for the kind of job and workplace in which you can succeed. You can evaluate any job to see how well it fits your guidelines. You can remodel your present position, explore new career directions, carve out a new function within the same organization, or look for a new job in an organization where more of your career guidelines can be met. Once you recognize the factors that work best for you, you can create them in any situation.

FOUR PLACES TO GO

1. A Remodeled Job

Recovering people often leave a good job for a bad reason. Your present job may offer many favorable career and recovery factors, but lack the spark that keeps you motivated. Before you leave, try pumping new life into the old job by adding the missing ingredient. If you have done your list-making tasks, you can identify what you need to make your job sizzle again. Here is the example of a recovering prescription drug addict who needed one factor to make her job exciting again: she needed *recognition.*

Sharon's job as marketing director for a mining development company gives her a chance to be creative while satisfying her keen business sense. The company owner takes interest in Sharon's recovery program and often talks with her about recovery principles.

Well-known and respected in the industry, Sharon uses her many contacts to uncover new business prospects. Then she researches and plans new business presentations, writes brochures, and makes initial telephone or correspondence contacts. She prepares the audiovisuals and briefs the owner prior to the first company/client meeting.

Despite doing all this ground-laying work, Sharon was never asked to make or attend an actual presentation. The owner always handled client contacts alone. Before she began her recovery, Sharon did not mind being excluded. She did not want other people to see how insecure she was. In addition, her codependent work relationship with her boss cast her in a supporting role, and she felt comfortable staying out of the limelight.

In recovery, however, Sharon's attitude changed. Her hard-won self-esteem needed a way to shine. She needed to let others know that she, not her boss, came up with those brilliant ideas and put together those snazzy presentations. The longer she went without recognition, the more unsatisfied she felt. Finally, she made up her mind to change jobs. But before she went job hunting, she decided to see if she could add that missing factor to an otherwise interesting and rewarding job.

She suggested to her boss that she attend the next presentation, where she could explain background information and he could give the main selling points. She emphasized that she might know some facts and figures that would help close the sale. To her surprise, her boss agreed. When they began making presentations as a team, Sharon's restlessness disappeared.

Does your job need remodeling? Would a change of one or two factors make you more satisfied? It is worth a try. By taking time to write your lists and discover what you need, you can find ways to create an exciting, fulfilling work environment.

2. A New Career

Talents and interests that were hidden by drinking and using other drugs often surface in recovery. Maybe, like many recovering people, you feel you don't know how to do anything else, or you believe your present job is the only one you can get. Maybe you fear change because of financial insecurity, or you don't know where to look for new job opportunities.

If you have made your lists, you can use those guidelines to research new careers. Decide what careers offer the most factors compatible with your needs. You can look through job information from the United States Department of Labor, read books about every career field from aerospace to zoology, attend career-change classes and workshops, talk to people in careers that interest you, visit the local college or university career testing office, or consult a qualified career counselor.

Many recovering people find a new career when they return to high school or college, and they realize that certain classes interest them more than others. As these classes stimulate them intellectually and emotionally, they begin to use talents that were once wasted. They may realize that their present career underutilizes their abilities — no wonder they get bored! Ron is an example of a recovering person who found a new career when he returned to college.

You never see Ron without a smile. His likeable manner helped his career as a systems analyst, even though he did not have a college degree. As Group Manager of Application Development for a growing city, Ron earned a healthy salary and looked ahead to a comfortable retirement. But something was missing.

"When what I was doing became routine and boring, I'd move up to the next level. Some people find ways within their occupation to meet their needs, but I reached a level and burned out on it, and then I had to move on to the next level to keep me interested. I had the choice of staying with the City, spending the next seventeen years waiting for retirement, versus taking the risk of finding something I will feel good about doing for the next seventeen years. I decided that, if you're going to work for another fifteen to twenty years, you may as well take the chance and do something interesting."

Ron sought the help of a career counselor, who gave him standard work-type, skills, aptitude, and interest-inventory tests. He scored high on business/professional and technical/professional (interests that fit his present job), with engineering, science, and math ranking second. Those tests confirmed his idea that engineering might use more of his skills and interests, and they helped shortcut the process of finding a new career direction.

He resigned his position and used his retirement fund to finance his education. But Ron found that talking about changing careers was easy; actually *doing* it created a lot of fear. "I thought that fear of economic insecurity had gone. But I spent the better part of three

months waking up with an overwhelming fear telling me
that I was crazy to give up everything I'd earned and
worked for. I'd quickly push that down and move on.
Now I'm at the point where I rarely, if ever, wake up that
way."

Fear fades as his skills and interests are stimulated. He
finds that math and science use thinking processes that
"turn me on." He says, "These six months have done
more for my self-esteem and self-worth than my computer career ever did."

Ron credits therapy and AA with helping him overcome fear and realize his ideas. "I was at a place in my
program, at three and a half years in sobriety, where I
would have thrown away my career because I was in that
much pain, and I could have impulsively quit my job. I
chose to face those feelings and memories, and work
with a lot of intensive therapy for a year. At the end of
that, I felt free to make major life changes, without any
hidden agenda. If I hadn't done that work, I would now
be in a lot of self-created misery.

"Recovery gave me the freedom to act on my values
and to throw away the scripts other people gave me. It's
a spiritual awakening — the whole process of self-
discovery and going back to school. It's really fun. I feel
like a kid again."

Before you scoff at the notion of returning to school, answer
this question honestly: Do you want to spend the next twenty
years doing what you are doing now? Remember, even if a
course doesn't point you in another career direction, at least it
will stimulate unused brain cells and will get your adrenaline
flowing.

3. A New Job Within the Same Organization
You might have the wrong job in the right company. For
example, you might be working for a major insurance company

that encourages recovery. It practices honesty, openness, clear communications, shared feelings, and high ethical standards. Nevertheless, as an insurance salesperson, you feel overly stressed by the job requirements, such as making cold calls, working nights and weekends, and meeting sales quotas. A different job, perhaps in research or marketing, could put you in a less stressful position within the same company.

Large companies with an equal-employment opportunity program look for employees they can promote from within. They may advertise job openings in a company newsletter and post job notices on department bulletin boards. When you see an opening that interests you, you have an advantage over outsiders because you can walk into that department and talk to the person in charge of hiring. With your career and recovery guidelines in mind, you can evaluate the job opening for how it fits your needs. You can also explain any problems or conflicts that developed in your current position and assure your prospective supervisor that they will not reoccur.

Moving into another department or changing jobs goes more smoothly when you know someone on the inside. Whom can you use as a resource? That person undoubtedly knows what the new job entails and how to get on the inside hiring track. You don't need to beat around the bush; take the person to lunch and ask directly, "I'm interested in the job opening in your department. What can you tell me about the position? What kind of person are they looking for?"

Your contact person might introduce you informally to the hiring authority. Even a quick "hello" and a handshake can convey your interest and enthusiasm. Then, when your formal application reaches the boss's desk, it has a better chance of being well received.

Making such inter-organizational changes is a typical move for supervisors, managers, and professionals. Often, horizontal moves can easily be made to another department where the same skills and experience are needed and the recovering person will feel more comfortable.

4. A New Job in a New Organization

Most of us dislike job hunting because we think of it as one rejection after another. As recovering persons, we may take these rejections personally. We begin to think ominous thoughts about never finding a job, always being underpaid and underappreciated, never being worth anything, losing the respect of our friends and family, and ending up alone and forgotten.

But job hunting can be an adventure in self-discovery. It can give you new self-knowledge, new appreciation of your gifts and abilities, new insight into your needs and wants, and gratitude for being who and what you are. *How* you job hunt makes the difference between defeat and victory.

Many recovering people feel so guilty and embarrassed about their disease that they believe no employer will ever want to hire them. When they get up enough courage to look for a job, they go about it like beggars looking for a handout. They want someone to *give* them a job. This attitude takes away the job hunter's power and puts it in the hands of employers. The job hunter no longer controls whether he or she will work or not; the employer does. Without personal power, the job hunter feels frustrated, humiliated. That feeling communicates a negative attitude to potential employers and drowns out the positive assets you can bring to the job.

Your attitude changes when you accept yourself — disease and all — as a worthwhile person. You look, not for a handout or acceptance, but for the place where you belong. And you will not settle for less than you deserve. As counselor Jonathan Hartshorne puts it:

> To the degree that I love myself and acknowledge my deservability, I open up to accept and create a quality work life. If my internal self-talk says, "I'm worthless, I don't deserve anything," the greatest opportunity could come along, but I'm not eligible for it because I disqualify myself.

Many people have done far worse things than you ever imagined. Many bear far deeper emotional scars, far more hurtful memories. Many carry physical and mental handicaps more debilitating than yours. Many such "unemployables" now manage profitable companies, heal the sick, perform on concert stages, govern cities and states, and sit on the boards of directors of major corporations. They learned to overcome their feelings of inadequacy, take the chip off their shoulder, and go out and find their place.

THE RIGHT WAY TO FIND A JOB

You find your place in the work world by moving carefully through the four basic stages any serious job hunter should take. These stages are:

1. Find out who you are and what you have to sell to prospective employers.

2. Find out what the marketplace needs and how you can fill those needs.

3. Find people to talk to in those organizations.

4. Present yourself well to those persons who can hire you.

Find Out Who You Are and What You Have to Sell To Prospective Employers

Finding out who you are takes time, honesty, and courage. It means asking yourself tough questions that you may not want to face. But, unless you know yourself and what you are seeking, you cannot find satisfaction in any job.

If you are following a Twelve Step program, you may have already probed into your motives, values, strengths, and shortcomings. The Fourth Step tells you to inventory yourself, and your work-related issues should be part of that process. If you have not done a Fourth Step on your work life, now is the time.

You can look back over past successes and failures and ask yourself such questions as:

- What kind of work do I enjoy doing?
- What have I not had a chance to do that I would like to do in the future?
- What kind of people do I like working with?
- What, besides income, do I want from my job?
- Why do I lose interest in one job and seek satisfaction from another?
- What kinds of choices have I made that have worked out well for me?
- What do I expect from a job that I have not yet found?
- How important is my job to my self-esteem?
- What problems do I frequently encounter on a job?
- What have others praised about my work, and what have they criticized?
- What values, such as honesty, simplicity, and humor, do I need from my boss and co-workers?
- If I could choose my ideal job, what qualities would it have?

These are nonjudgmental questions, with no right or wrong answers. They help you look at yourself, your motives, and your values. Taking time to answer such questions helps you understand the role that work plays in your life beyond the obvious factors of salary, location, hours, benefits, and duties. Perhaps most importantly, it shows you what job situations to avoid.

Sometimes we need help to look deeply into our innermost selves. Another person, such as your sponsor, counselor, or a former employer, may give you insights that you overlooked. With your answers already written, you can listen to the other person's views and add their comments.

The next assignment on this road to self-discovery is an inventory of your work skills, personal skills, and positive traits. You can probably list your work skills fairly quickly, but you may draw a blank when you try to list your personal skills and positive traits. Often, the recovering person's confidence droops so low that he or she cannot see any positives to offer an employer. In that case, someone else, particularly a career or work life counselor, or a close friend, can help you discover your selling points. Professional career counseling can also help you look beyond the job label you have always worn.

Sometimes job hunters fall into the trap of labeling themselves. They think, "I'm a teacher," or "I'm a computer engineer," or "I'm a retail salesperson" and assume their title is a permanent classification. Unfortunately, self-labeling shuts the door on many opportunities. Every job or career consists of dozens of skills that apply to other functions. In addition, your personal skills, attributes, and interests are likely to qualify you to move into other career areas.

An advertising agency account executive who was looking for a new job with greater advancement potential had labeled himself an "account executive" and looked only for jobs with that label. Since he worked exclusively on accounts in the banking industry, he further qualified his label as "account executive for a financial institution." This self-labeling cut him off from dozens of jobs in which his experience would have been valuable.

He listed his skills: market research, budget analysis and forecasting, product development, client and agency liaison, report writing, intradepartmental information dissemination, document preparation, formal presentations, scheduling, and work flow management. Any one of these skills opens the door to a new job title, such as "market researcher," "budget analyst and forecaster," or "new business development specialist." Looking at his skills in this manner gave him a wide-angle view of his career opportunities, instead of the limited, one-label view that left him only one option.

"That's fine for the experienced person," a common argument goes. "But I've been out of the work force so long that I don't have any marketable skills." This reaction may reveal low self-esteem with a tinge of self-pity, and that attitude can bog you down in problems, rather than bring solutions.

Everyone Has Experience that Someone Else Needs

One housewife I know had not worked outside the home in over ten years when she decided to enter the job market again. At first, looking at her lack of business experience, she moaned that she couldn't find a job. However, as the mother of an active teenager, she had participated in parent-teacher activities, headed fund-raising drives, organized sporting events, and directed service groups at school and church. When her son had volunteered as an aide to a city counselor, she had met a handful of city political figures.

Looking at her personal skills, she realized that she had fund-raising ability, organizational skills, and important contacts that many organizations need. The former "unemployable" housewife now works as a fund-raiser for a privately endowed university where her skills keep the financial coffers full and new projects feasible.

As you remember what you have done in the past, you will recall details that can create an impressive list of skills. Your personal traits add more sales points. Here's a sample of the kinds of questions to ask yourself to expand your list of qualifications:

- Do you learn quickly?
- Are you patient?
- Can you deal well with irate customers?
- Do you like to travel?
- Are you a hard worker?
- Do you have high energy and endurance?
- Can you follow directions?
- Are you good with details?

- Are you neat and well-groomed?
- Are you eager and willing to learn new skills and assume new responsibilities?
- Do you have a pleasant telephone voice?
- Do you have a good manual dexterity?
- Are you one of those rare persons who can find a solution to a seemingly impossible dilemma when everyone else is pretty much stymied?
- Do you have leadership ability?
- Are you forceful, determined, persistent?

Whatever your personal qualities, you are likely to be a desirable employee to *someone, somewhere,* no matter how spotty your work history or incomplete your experience.

These skills, the ones you have already acquired from your education and work or life experience, plus your personal traits, will add up to an impressive list of selling points.

Sometimes, deep in the back of our minds, we dream of becoming something we have always wanted to be. Dreams can be fun and they can help us find the missing ingredients in our work life. Many persons fulfill their dreams by studying and practicing, by starting their own business, or by taking the risk of doing something new. Others hang on to unreachable, unrealistic dreams that take the pleasure out of their present career and cut them off from the satisfaction of a new direction.

Are you being realistic? If your driver's license has been suspended, you cannot work as a taxicab driver or truck driver. If you have a prison record, you will have difficulty getting hired for a job that requires bondable employees. If you have poor physical health or low energy, you cannot effectively compete for jobs that require physical exertion.

By recognizing your limitations, you can make realistic choices and practical decisions. You can find a place in which you can do well, not a place full of disappointment and failure. You have had enough bad things happen to you; give yourself a break. Find broad areas of interest, then learn what jobs within those areas you can do successfully. Set yourself up for success.

Find Out What the Marketplace Needs And How You Can Fill Those Needs

Now you can begin looking for the place where your skills and your attributes are needed and can be used, appreciated, and rewarded.

You want to consider first those broad career areas in which your interests and skills apply, such as banking, fashion, construction, sales, public relations, or health. Also study industry trends and anticipate businesses where employment demand is growing

Multiply Your Options

Rather than limit employment opportunities to an area in which you already have experience, broaden your horizons by considering at least three others. The advertising agency account executive who thought he was limited to another agency with banking clients multiplied his career options by listing these other possible areas where his qualifications might apply:

- Marketing department of financial institution
- Research department of stock brokerage or market consulting firm
- Management consulting firm specializing in financial planning or organizational restructuring

When you add up all the skills you have acquired, you can multiply your options by finding several different areas in which those skills can be utilized. You can then begin to locate particular organizations within those areas and find out what they need.

Analyze the Market

According to James P. Challenger, president of the Chicago-based corporate outplacement firm of Challenger, Gray & Christmas, Inc.:

What you look at is what the marketplace wants and then figure out how your talents can benefit them. Talk to people and find out what they need, then fit your background into their needs. It's much easier to assess your abilities against something that is viable than something that is nonexistent.

Companies want what they are now lacking. But you won't know what they want until you pick up the telephone and talk to them. Once you find out what a company lacks, you can point out how your skills and experience can fill the void.

Further, says Challenger:

If you're a recovering alcoholic or addict, you talk to smaller companies because they will buy talent that a larger company won't. They will be willing to put up with what might be a problem, when a larger company might not. Big companies won't stick their neck out and hire a recovering alcoholic or addict. But a small company can figure out what to do with them.

Look for smaller companies within your areas of interest. You find them *by doing your homework*. Once you have decided on three or four broad areas of interest, locate those companies that need your skills. Read industry newspapers and magazines, follow the business news in your daily paper, consult back issues of business magazines, search *The Yellow Pages*, follow classified ads, talk to friends and business associates, and attend industry workshops and conventions. If you are thinking about changing careers, you can arrange information-gathering interviews with knowledgeable experts who can discuss the new career's pros and cons.

These fact-finding activities will net you a list of companies and names of key persons to contact. Then keep adding to and updating your list as new leads develop. You will need a *long* list of potential employers to generate the number of interviews that result in the right job. One job-finding organization suggests that you make at least *ten employer contacts every day.*[2] Challenger, Gray & Christmas requires that, if you are under forty years of age, you have *four interviews a day.* If you are between forty and fifty-three, or over fifty years of age, *two a day.* "That's how you get a job," says Challenger. "Getting a job correlates with the numbers. The more interviews you go on, the faster you'll get hired."

Keep Records

You will be collecting scores of names, addresses, and telephone numbers. You will be contacting dozens of employers. You will be following up those contacts with telephone calls and letters. To keep all of this information organized and available, you will need to keep accurate records.

One important list keeps track of leads, including who gave you the lead, whom to contact, and what action you took. Headings might look like this:

Contact Person	*Lead*	*Action Taken*
Mary Petersen Anderville Electric 2913 Parklane 293-8765	Gordon Monroe Sunland Electrical Supply 56790 Union 345-7786	Interview 8/5 at 4 p.m. Two referrals

Another list shows general activity, like this:

Date	*Company*	*Contact Person*	*Action*	*Result*	*Next Step*
8/16	Archer 53 Park	Mr. Simpson (357-8712)	Int'view	Wants me to call Tuesday	Call 8/19

As your leads list develops and you get caught up in job-finding activity, you can easily forget two vital points. First, not every company is the right environment for a recovering person. Second, somewhere on these lists is the company best for you. It is the place that needs you and the place you need. As you continue your search, you will find that right fit, and it will feel good for both the company and you.

Find People to Talk to in Those Organizations

People Hire People They Like

Employers don't hire strangers. They don't hire resumés. They hire people they meet face-to-face. Someone makes the final hiring decision. The closer you get to that someone, the more likely you will land the job you want. Your task then becomes finding the right person to talk to, the man or woman who can hire you. Here are four tips for finding that person.

1. Go to the Top

Your first step should take you to appropriate departments (purchasing, marketing, accounting, shipping) within those businesses where you have interests and strengths. Ask for the names of the heads of those departments and *talk only to them.*

You learn names simply by asking whoever answers the telephone, "Who is the head of the sales department?" You can then speak directly to that person, write an approach letter and follow up with a telephone call, or go directly to the person's office and ask to talk to him or her. This direct-to-the-top approach bypasses the personnel department where applications and resumés are filed away.

You can talk to anybody if you really want to. You may be pleasantly surprised at how easily your telephone call goes through. Nevertheless, once you reach the hiring person, you will have only a few minutes to present yourself effectively; the entire interview may take place in a sudden, three-minute telephone conversation.

Try to sound relaxed and comfortable, not hurried and nervous. To help you remember what you want to say, you might write a script or outline of the key points you want to make.

Perhaps a friend or counselor will help you rehearse your pitch until you feel confident.

2. Start in Your Own Backyard

You can build your contact list by talking to friends, family members, business associates, and former classmates. When you know someone who knows someone, you can more easily reach the person in charge and get a chance to interview. I got my first job as a junior copywriter when my landlady, a media buyer, arranged an interview with an associate creative director at the same ad agency.

When you contact old friends, they may remember you as a person who lived on alcohol or other drugs. You may need to tell them briefly about your past ("I was acting that way because I was drinking too much") and what you did ("I got help and now I'm getting my life straightened out"). You need not weave a long, sad story; that's not your message and the other person is probably not interested. A simple one-sentence explanation will suffice. Stress the positive; you have done something about your problem and can now make a meaningful contribution.

Then they will want to know why you are contacting them ("I am looking for a job in sales, and I know you work for a company that has a terrific product") and how they can help ("Can you tell me whom to telephone about possible openings in the sales department?"). To help you, your friend will need a brief run-down of your experience ("I have five years' experience selling recreational vehicles and three years with computers. I'm very good at demonstrating how a product works"). If he or she gives you the name of a person or company to contact, be sure to let your friend know the results of that referral.

3. Try the Old-Fashioned Way

Often the best job leads pop up right under your nose, in the newspaper. Articles about successful businesses and news about executive promotions or plant expansions almost always include the names and titles of key company figures. Where there is a promotion, there is a vacancy left by the promoted person. Where there is an expansion, there can be hundreds of potential jobs. You can add the names mentioned in the article or news item to your leads list, then contact those persons.

Even the classified "Help Wanted" section can turn up a promising job lead. As you read each listing, you will see job opportunities where your skills match. Even if you meet only one or two qualifications, you should take a chance and make that contact. Your interests and attributes may impress the employer more than your experience. In addition, companies that are actively hiring often have openings in other departments. Also in this section you can check the "Jobs Wanted" listings for any persons whose background is similar to yours. You might contact those persons with the idea of sharing information and leads.

If you belong to a professional or business association that circulates a newsletter, you can easily find the names of up-and-coming persons and companies to contact. You can also respond to classified "Positions Available" listings. If a name and telephone number are listed, you might telephone and pre-sell your qualifications before you send your resumé.

Although only thirteen percent of job holders got their jobs through newspaper want ads,[3] you might join the employed ranks by using that method. But don't rely on the "Help Wanted" ads as your primary or sole source of job leads. These listings should be considered a small part of your overall job-finding plan.

4. Avoid the Letter/Resumé/Wastebasket Method

Says Challenger,

> As far as writing an approach letter and sending a resumé, forget it. The letter goes in the wastebasket, and the resumé is only a crutch. Yes, you might need a resumé, because some people ask for it. But we stopped letter-writing as a mode for getting a job seventeen or

eighteen years ago. Companies are inundated with letters. It's the worst possible thing you can do. It's the personal contact — the voice, the face — if I like you, I might think about hiring you.

Nevertheless, other career and placement specialists believe the letter/resumé method works effectively. Says Susan Silvano of Career Management International, "Write the proper approach letter, follow up with a phone call, then go and discuss your strengths. If you present yourself well, this method works for everybody."

What doesn't work is sending out hundreds of letters and never following up. The employer either will not answer your letter or will respond with a form rejection letter. Only when you take the initiative to telephone and ask for an interview do you get a chance for a face-to-face meeting.

Sometimes the letter/resumé method is your only means of making contact. You may be unable to reach the hiring person by telephone; you may want to avoid expensive long-distance telephone rates; or you may have to answer a "Help Wanted" ad by sending your resumé to an anonymous box number.

In these cases, you should write an approach letter that tells why you want to work for that company. You set the right tone when you know something good about the company and refer to it in your letter. You score extra points if you know something good about the person to whom you are writing and explain why you want to see that individual. Your letter should then point out places in which your skills and experience will help reach the organization's goals. You end with a request for an interview and assurance that you will telephone in four or five days to arrange a convenient time. Include your mailing address and a daytime telephone number, in case the employer wants to reach you.

All this researching, networking, list-making, writing, and telephoning can become discouraging. You may feel as though you have wasted your time. Or you can feel afraid of actually walking into a strange company and talking to a strange person.

But there comes a time when you have to go out and do it. These preparations lay the foundation for effective interviewing; and effective interviewing is what gets you hired.

Present Yourself Well to Those Persons Who Can Hire You

Let me say it again: People hire people they like. Therefore, you want to emphasize qualities that employers like and deemphasize those they dislike. Often recovering people feel so uncomfortable about their disease that they say too much about the past. Recovering people need to reduce the fact that they are different and increase the fact that they have something positive to offer.

Don't Lead with the Negative

In support group meetings, aftercare sessions, and conversations with friends, recovering people talk openly about their past escapades and their newly found health and spirituality. They consider their recovery their biggest asset, and it undoubtedly is. But, during an interview, though the topic of your disease may eventually have to come up, it should not be your opening statement. Carefully choose the time and manner in which to share private information.

A few recovering persons wear a chip on their shoulder. The first thing they say to an employer is, "I'm an alcoholic, so you won't want to hire me." Their defensive attitude immediately makes the employer wary. If you are negative about yourself, the employer can think only that you would be a negative influence on the job.

Anybody can dredge up reasons that make him or her unemployable. All of us have our problems, *but don't talk yourself out of a job.* An enthusiastic, eager-to-work, I-love-my-career attitude can get you hired, even when your qualifications don't match those of other applicants. It is okay to get fired up and excited about a job opening. It is *not* okay to sound bored, indifferent, unenthusiastic, or defensive.

141

Emphasize Your Strengths

When you meet a prospective employer, you want to show-case your strengths, your skills, your experience, your enthusiasm, your good health, your achievements, your reliability—the positives. Says Silvano:

> Present yourself through the things you are proud of — the things you've done at home, in the community, or in business — and give the results of those things. Then the discussion of addiction, or any other problem, is a small part of your interview.

Often, you can complete the interview and get hired without ever referring to your disease. If it comes up during the interview, for example, to explain a very erratic work history, the best solution is to handle it briefly and conversationally, stressing that you have taken care of that problem and no longer drink alcohol or use other drugs. As smoothly as possible, shift the discussion back to the benefits you offer the employer.

Employers want to know only two things: What strengths do you offer that will increase the company's profitability? And, what can you give the company that it now lacks? Everything you say, whether by telephone or in person, should be directed toward answering those questions. Any other comments you add should be made only to "warm up" the interview and establish rapport.

To focus on your strengths, imagine that *you* are the interviewer and ask yourself what qualities you want in the person you hire.[4] You can even write them on a note card or pad so you remember to mention those points in your interview. You will want to cover such selling points as:

- how much you increased sales
- how much money you saved the company
- what new ideas you suggested that worked well
- why you were promoted and how often
- whom you trained and brought up within the company

- how you contributed to setting new goals
- how you guided policy changes
- what responsibilities you assumed that were not included in your job description
- what "impossible" tasks you were able to accomplish
- how you expanded your job, your territory, your client list
- how much production you accomplished in a given time period
- what compliments clients paid you
- how clients benefited from your performance
- what extra responsibilities, such as union representative or charity coordinator, you were elected to or nominated for
- what awards, such as Employee of the Month, you won
- what types of equipment you can operate that others cannot
- what double-duty jobs you can do, such as cook/counter person, driver/stock person, media buyer/account executive, or teacher/job placement coordinator.

As the interview progresses, you may hear clues that indicate a potential need. For example, the sales manager might comment that he has an experienced salesperson out in the field who has a top-notch sales record. The clue? The salesperson is out of the office all day. The company needs someone who can handle inside sales, correspondence, and record keeping.

Or, the creative director says that all her copywriters can turn out five ads a day. The clue? Those copywriters are overworked! The agency needs a writer who can relieve some of the pressure. Asking questions about the organization and listening to the interviewer's remarks will help you discover areas of need that your strengths can fill.

❋ ❋ ❋ ❋ ❋

Not everyone knows how to interview well. Many people have not learned to write their resumé or talk clearly and confidently on the telephone. Some don't know how to dress correctly, write a thank-you letter, or respond to a "Help Wanted" ad. These job-finding skills don't come naturally, but they can be learned.

If you feel unsure of your job-finding skills or if you have been job hunting for a month without an offer, you should consider getting professional assistance. You can get a wealth of information and guidance from career counselors and placement firms who specialize in getting you ready for that all-important interview or from such resources as job-preparedness classes at vocational/technical schools; placement centers at colleges and universities; employment offices of city, state, and federal agencies, such as the Comprehensive Employment and Training Agency (CETA), the Job Training Division of your state Labor Department, and your state vocational rehabilitation department.

Another way to learn job-finding skills is through the Job Club, an organization of small, counselor-assisted groups that meet to share job leads and find employment. If your community offers a Job Club, it may be available through one of the resources above or alcohol/drug treatment programs offered by a university or mental health facility.

You can list a dozen skills, write an impressive resumé, and set up a hundred hot interviews. But if you don't present yourself well over the telephone and in interviews, you will pound the job-hunting trail for endless months. If you have not found a job after sincere effort, it is time to ask yourself one serious question: *Are you failing to get a job because you are a recovering person or because you are not presenting yourself effectively?* Your sponsor, minister, counselor, and recovering friends can help you answer honestly. You cannot change your disease, but you can change plenty about your presentation.

You can stop the rejection cycle by taking a break for two or three weeks, getting the training you need, and starting fresh. With the right presentation, you will find the place that needs you, the place where you can make a contribution. You will find the right "fit" for recovery.

As a recovering person, you might ask your Higher Power for help and guidance, and trust that you will find the way.

ENDNOTES
Chapter Six

1. Adapted with permission from a seminar, "Achieving Sustained High Performance," by Jerry L. Fletcher, Ph.D.

2. Nathan H. Azrin and Victoria A. Besalel, *Finding a Job* (Berkeley, Calif.: 1982), 19.

3. Azrin and Besalel, *Finding a Job*, 54. Taken from a Bureau of Labor Statistics national survey, 1975.

4. Richard A. Payne, *How to Get a Better Job Quicker* (New York: Taplinger's Press, Inc., 1987). Used with permission in the *Executive Female*, July/August 1988 edition, 46-50.

CHAPTER SEVEN

TOUGH QUESTIONS AND SMART ANSWERS

Recovering people can stumble over interview questions that other job seekers take in stride, such as "Why did you leave your last job?" They know an honest answer may ruin their chances of getting hired. They don't want to lie, but they don't know what to say. If their discomfort signals a warning to the interviewer, the job opportunity may disappear. If you have had that uncomfortable experience, you probably dread interviewing, and that fear may prevent you from expressing yourself clearly and confidently.

Other situations may throw you off balance and put you in an awkward position. For example, pre-employment practices such as taking a lie-detector test or submitting to drug screening can seem monumental barriers. Lack of references or recommendations can make you appear less eligible. With competition for jobs as keen as it is today, you should not seem anything less than one-hundred-percent employable.

Here are some of the toughest questions and situations recovering people face when they go job hunting. You will feel more self-assured by taking time to think through and rehearse how you will respond to such questions and how you will act when in these situations. If you feel uncertain about how to handle any of these questions, ask another recovering person who is presently employed for further suggestions.

How Should I Fill Out a Job Application That Asks About Alcohol or Other Drugs?

There are three workable approaches to this question.

One avoids filling out a job application by going straight to the person who can hire you. With this method, you research and select the companies you want to approach. You ask for the name of the head of the appropriate department, the person in a position to hire you, and you circumvent the personnel department. You discuss first the company's needs and how you can fill them, then you honestly and briefly explain any concerns about your past, and finally, refocus the interview on your strengths. If the employer asks a blunt question, like, "Do you use drugs?" you might say something like this:

"No, I don't use drugs. I'm very healthy, clear-headed, and reliable, and I will give you one-hundred-percent effort on every assignment."

If you are subsequently hired, you can fill out an application and write "N/A"(Not Applicable) in those troublesome spaces. If you are not hired, you will not have to worry about the application form at all.

A second approach is to leave any space *blank* if your response would automatically disqualify you or if the answer needs your verbal explanation. You might decide to leave several questions blank, such as those that refer to your age, your bondability, your salary requirements, or your reason for leaving your last job. You can discuss these questions in a personal interview, without revealing your private business to every curious eye. If you are subsequently hired, you can write "N/A" in those blanks or write candid answers, assured that your employer already knows your history.

A third approach is to answer application questions truthfully, filling in all the spaces, leaving nothing to the employer's imagination. This approach may disqualify you from many jobs; many companies will not consider an applicant who admits to alcoholism or drug addiction, even if the person has been clean and sober for years. Other companies look for the best qualified person, regardless of past mistakes. At least they will give you a chance to explain how you straightened yourself out and how you can now contribute more effectively to the organization. This is the kind of company in which you can succeed.

The only wrong approach is lying. Although many employers do not take the time to verify application answers, some go to extensive efforts to check a candidate's background.

No matter what you do, some companies absolutely will not hire a recovering person, even the best-qualified applicant. If the department head, foreman, or manager shows a hostile attitude toward recovering people, you can cross that company off your list. Chalk it up to experience and consider yourself lucky; that company is the wrong place for a recovering person.

If you feel a bit depressed because you struck out at one place, you can turn to your sponsor, counselor, or support group for a good pep talk. Somewhere out there is a job where you will be needed, appreciated, and rewarded. It might be the next place you contact.

How Should I Explain Long Periods of Unemployment?

Sometimes recovering people have long blank periods in their work history. Perhaps they disappeared on Skid Row or into a mental institution or behind prison walls. Now, years later, they must try to account for those time periods.

You cannot explain satisfactorily in the two-inch space on an application form. You cannot do it in a three-minute telephone conversation. It must be done in a face-to-face discussion with the person who can hire you. Just as answered in the first question, going directly to that person puts you in the best position. He or she might ask what you have been doing for the few years since your last job. Your answer should explain briefly what the problem was and what you did to overcome it, then shift the subject back to the positive attributes you can bring to the job. For example, you might say:

> At one time I had a drinking problem that interfered with my career. I got into treatment and now I don't have that problem. In fact, I don't drink at all. Now I am enthusiastic about getting back to work and making up for lost time. I'm sure I can ... (Continue by explaining what you can do for the company.)

When recovering people feel unsure of themselves, they might make "killer comments," like this, that crush any chance they have of being hired:

> I was a cocaine addict and robbed a bank and ended up in prison. I'm sure you won't consider hiring me now that you know I'm an ex-con.

Or ...

> Everywhere I go, people say the same thing. They don't want to hire me because I'm an alcoholic. You're just like all the rest.

Or ...

> I couldn't get a job for over a year because my previous boss bad-mouthed me every place I tried to get hired. He's probably told you about me already, right?

These resentful, self-pitying statements instantly alienate the employer and shut off communication. They keep the recovering person locked in the past, doomed to repeat the same mistakes. If you suspect that you might be saying too much or saying the wrong things, you might ask your counselor or an employed friend to role-play interviews. You can tape record the sessions and play them back to hear your own "killer comments" and thus eliminate destructive thinking and speaking.

What If I Can't Provide a Reference?

Some hiring decisions, particularly for professional and managerial positions, are based on references. Recovering people may discover that previous employers refuse to recommend them; the applicant loses out because his or her job file is never completed. Or a former boss may give an unfavorable reference. A bad reference is worse than no reference, because employers fear that you will repeat the same damaging behavior.

You can try several strategies and see what works best. Ordinarily, job applicants list immediate supervisors as references, as well as owners, managers, or administrators who can attest to their qualifications. If these persons refuse to recommend you or if they provide only unfavorable references, then you can turn to co-workers, persons in other departments, business associates, counselors, former teachers, a sponsor, minister, principal, warden, judge, doctor — anybody whose job title reflects good judgment and business experience. Ideally, these referring persons have known you long enough to say good things about the quality of your work, your reliability, and your assets as an employee.

You should tell your references to expect a few telephone calls from potential employers during the next month or two, while you are job hunting. You should ask them to submit any necessary letters of recommendation as quickly as possible, so you don't miss a hiring deadline. Or you can request an open letter of recommendation — "To whom it may concern" — that you can photocopy and carry in your job folder (along with extra copies of your resumé, certificates, diplomas, and other relevant documents).

Before you list anyone as a reference, common sense and courtesy dictate that you ask the person for permission to use his or her name. You can ask what the person would say about you if a potential employer telephoned, and you can decide whether you want to use that person as a reference. You can brief the person on your qualifications and send him or her a brief summary of your skills, strengths, accomplishments, and successes.[1]

Another strategy is to ask a third party to arbitrate with any former employers who are giving you unfavorable recommendations or blackballing you. Perhaps you have been going from company to company, getting good interviews, then being turned down because of poor references. A career or placement counselor can step in and talk to those who are frustrating your efforts. You should be honest with the counselor when discussing what went wrong in your previous job, without blaming or bad-mouthing anyone The counselor can tell former employers that you are looking for a new job, that their poor references are making employment virtually impossible, and that your new attitude and behavior will make you a valuable employee in another company.

How Should I Explain Why I Left My Last Job?

An application form may ask, "Why did you leave your last job?" If your answer needs an explanation, you might choose to leave it blank and cover that question during the interview. Even if the application doesn't ask, your prospective employer might. It is a common interview question, and it needs an answer that puts you in the most favorable possible light.

You don't have to rake up old problems, open old wounds, retell old stories. You may have made some mistakes on your last job, but you are not going to make them again. The problems that existed in your old job do not exist here, and the people and circumstances are entirely different. *You are entirely different.* You are a new, sober person with new goals, new attitudes, and new behaviors that any employer would value. Instead of a long, sordid look at your past, the employer wants a short, reasonable explanation.

- If your boss hated you, don't say so.
- If you hated your boss, don't say so.
- If you were unfairly treated, don't say so.

Talking about these negatives only makes you seem difficult to get along with, and nobody wants an employee like that. As you think about your previous job, find two or three good qualities that you enjoyed and mention those. For instance, perhaps you liked the product you sold or the customers you serviced; perhaps you enjoyed traveling around the country or staying in the home office; perhaps you liked the hours or the physical layout of the plant. When you emphasize the positives, the potential employer believes that you are a positive person.

If you were dismissed, avoid the word "fired." It makes such a strongly negative impression that you will have difficulty turning the interview to a positive tone. You can give a simple, honest explanation that will satisfy the interviewer, then turn back to your interests and strengths. You might say:

> At that time, I had some personal problems and the job didn't work out. I've taken care of everything now, and I don't expect any problems in the future. I'm sure my experience . . .

Employers dislike evasiveness and appreciate honesty, but only when it is expressed in a professional manner. That is, you want to avoid embarrassing, soul-searching revelations about your past addictive behavior and how it influenced your last job. You want to stress that you have already dealt with the circumstances that adversely affected your last job and that you are enthusiastic about resuming your career and proving your value to this company. By exuding confidence and optimism, you show interviewers that you have the qualities they want.

Should I Consent to a Lie-Detector Test?
Should I Consent to Urine Testing?

Many employers use pre-employment tests to help screen job applicants. These may consist of polygraph (lie-detector) tests and/or urine tests to determine past or present on-the-job use of alcohol or controlled substances, such as amphetamines, barbiturates, cocaine, or opiates. You may consider such testing an invasion of privacy or a form of self-incrimination, or you may resent the employer's not taking your word for statements you make in an interview. However, testing will confirm your honesty and assure the employer that you told the truth. If the company considers such testing a condition of employment, you can either take the test or lose the job opportunity.

Before you agree to any pre-employment testing, however, you should know a few basic facts. Pre-employment lie-detector testing is no longer legal in the United States, except for federal, state, and local governments; companies that dispense drugs; security companies; and armored car services. Banned by a law that took effect 27 December 1988, lie-detector tests may no longer be used by private employers as a condition of employment or as the sole basis for adverse actions against employees. If you apply to an exempted company, however, you may be required to take a lie-detector test before you will be considered eligible to work for that employer.

Lie-detector tests, administered by licensed professionals, consist of three stages: (1) a forty- to forty-five-minute pre-test interview by the examiner, (2) a three-to-five-minute test, followed by a re-test to confirm findings, and (3) a brief post-test and re-testing if necessary. The idea is to produce a profile of the employee that the employer can use, along with other pre-employment measures, to determine employability.

According to Herman Romero, Owner and Chief Examiner of H & R Polygraph, the pre-test interview determines what questions will be asked in the test. During the pre-test, the examiner asks questions related to the applicant's job history and qualifications, as well as these five standard questions:

- Did you falsify your application with this employer?
- Have you stolen money or property from any employer?
- Have you been convicted of any crime?
- Have you used alcohol or other drugs while on the job?
- Do you have any citations, such as DUI or DWI, that affect your qualifications to drive a vehicle?

This pre-test interview lets you know what kinds of questions will be asked on the test and gives you a chance to think about and change your answers. For example, you might admit that you used amphetamines to stay awake while driving an eighteen-wheeler cross-country. In the test, the examiner might ask, "Have you worked under the influence of any drugs *other than amphetamines?*" You can then truthfully answer no.

During the pre-test, the examiner should take time to explain the procedure and answer questions. The applicant must sign a release stating that he or she is taking the test voluntarily. If the applicant feels coerced into taking the test, fear and anger may elicit responses that can be interpreted as untruthful. If the applicant has recently been ill, he or she may feel edgy, and test responses will be unreliable. You should tell the examiner about any feelings or physical condition that may influence your test, and you should request rescheduling if you do not feel calm, healthy, and well-prepared.

The test itself takes only a few minutes. If the examiner notices a response that appears to be a lie, he or she must bring that response to your attention. You will be asked to clarify your response so the examiner can rephrase the question on a re-test. "If the recovering person is candid," says Romero, "the employer has a better handle on how to trust this individual. It becomes a very helpful thing. Tell it the way it is, because you will be a better person for it anyway, and you won't have that secret to hide. Any time you hold something back, you take on more stress than you need to carry with you from day to day."

Like lie-detector testing, urinalysis documents a person's recovery. It proves you are not using drugs and therefore that you should be considered equally qualified with other job applicants.

"In many private businesses, the company's policy of pre-employment (urinalysis) testing is mandatory; it's a condition of employment," says Ron Smock, President and Owner of Drug Detection Services, Inc. He suggests you alert testing personnel to any medications you may have taken during the past week (prescription or over-the-counter) or that you were given during treatment, if you were recently released. Some treatment facilities administer medications, particularly tranquilizers, to help detoxify patients. These can stay in your bloodstream for an extended period of time and cause positive urinalysis results. If you test positive, you can explain to the employer and request a re-test. Remember, if you have nothing to hide, testing will help you prove it.

Should I Tell a Potential Employer that I Am In Recovery, Even If He or She Doesn't Ask?

You can feel sure that an employer will ask any questions that are relevant to the position for which you are applying. If you presented your strengths in a cordial, conversational way and if you answered questions clearly, simply, and honestly, you are under no obligation to bring up information that may adversely influence the interviewer's decision. It is possible that you can work for the company successfully for many years and never tell anybody about your disease if you don't want to.

When you know that the company requires pre-employment testing, however, your best move is to disclose anything you feel is necessary before the employer finds it out from test results. While you may be tempted to breathe a sigh of relief ("Thank goodness he didn't ask me about drugs!"), you don't want the employer to think you tried to hide something. You can bring up the subject by asking a question like this: "What kinds of pre-employment tests does your company require?" The interviewer can then explain any aptitude, personality, or alcohol or other drug tests that the company requires.

If you act ashamed, apologetic, evasive, or belligerent, the employer may get the impression that you have not dealt with your disease and that it continues to be a problem that will affect your job performance. On the other hand, if you show that you recognized your problem and took care of it, the employer can presume that you are fully capable of handling the job.

If you decide to talk about it, you need to go further and answer the employer's unspoken question, *What have you done to get your life in shape?* Now you should briefly talk about any therapy, counseling, or treatment you underwent, as well as support group or other recovery activities you regularly attend.

People like to know what to expect; they don't like finding out that a man or woman they are considering hiring did not tell them the truth or an important piece of information. If you are lucky, the employer will give you an opportunity to explain why the tests brought out facts that you did not mention in the interview. But the damage has already been done. The employer cannot help but wonder *what else are you keeping secret?*

What Should I Say About a Misdemeanor or Felony Conviction, a Prison Term, or Being on Probation?

Some mistakes can mean prison or probation or a lifetime blot on the person's honesty, reliability, and trustworthiness. A prison record or criminal conviction makes finding a job difficult, but not impossible. You will find the right job, even though you may need time to find a receptive employer.

Walter, a pharmacist, was convicted of a felony (fraud and theft of a controlled substance) and given eighteen months' suspended sentence and five years' probation. He tells his story this way:

> Trying to cover up and hide my disease got me in trouble. The grocery store chain I worked for started doing audits on Schedule II (controlled) drugs, and my store came up short. I was stealing, and I couldn't fake the numbers enough to cover myself.
>
> They fired me, and my wife and I moved to another state. I lied on my job application and got a job at a major discount retailer. That time, I went about a year without using. But I had no program, and I started using again. I thought I could get away with it, but it wasn't long before

157

there was a night audit and the numbers didn't add up. My supervisor called me in, and the security people and the police were there. I was taken downtown to jail. That was a Friday night; Monday, I checked into a treatment center, even though I had no insurance after being fired. I was introduced to AA there, and I've been attending ever since.

It was nineteen months before I found a full-time job. I did part-time work, taking a physical inventory for a hospital, doing relief work at a pharmacy, and helping a friend put in a computer system. I even looked for jobs outside of pharmacy. On my resumé and applications and in the interviews I always told the truth, and I got turned down for a lot of jobs.

Then, about a year ago, I finally heard of an opening at a big food center. The supervisor looked at my resumé and said, "This looks nice, but you've done a lot of skipping around." That's when I told him the whole story. He said, "I knew it already. I checked with the State Board of Pharmacy." He told me that, if I had lied, he wouldn't have hired me.

In general, people who know about recovery are very accepting. I told the store manager, too, and I am comfortable with that. But nobody else at work knows. If they hear about it and ask me, I won't hide it. When I accept life on life's terms, I do better.

Honesty and complete disclosure worked for Walter, and those qualities rank high with employers. But, if the employer doesn't ask, you are under no obligation to bring up personal facts that could cost you a job opportunity. If you are comfortable with yourself and with delivering that information, how and when you discuss your history can set a positive or negative tone that pervades the entire interview. Suggests Andrew Sherwood, Chairman of Goodrich & Sherwood, a New York based full-service human resource firm:

You've got to be candid. Answer every question you're asked in the interview. That doesn't mean you lead with your chin or offer it. Sooner or later in the employment process you are going to be asked to fill out an application, and you don't want to misrepresent on the application, because if you do, you are subject to termination at any point, once they find out.

Virtually everyone has had some kind of problem in their past, in their career. If you dwell on it too much or lead with it, you give people the impression that it will interfere with the job. In the formation of the initial relationship, people take the data they're given and form impressions. If that data is inaccurate or you're not honest right from the start, you leave yourself open for that person to be totally disillusioned and want to sever the relationship because it has no firm foundation.

In the opening minutes of the interview, you want to stress the successful parts of your career. You want to answer the employer's questions about your skills and experience, and you want to offer comments about accomplishments that show your career commitment. Then look for the appropriate moment to discuss your history, perhaps when the employer asks why you left your previous job or why you have not worked recently.

You might explain that there was a period in your life when alcohol or other drugs were a problem and that you had difficulties with the law. Then, in a matter-of-fact way, you can explain what you did to resolve that difficulty: you were incarcerated for a period of time; you were convicted and put on probation; you attended ninety meetings in ninety days of Alcoholics Anonymous and enrolled in an outpatient treatment program; you lost your driver's license for two years, attended driver's training school, and got counseling; your family participates in weekly counseling sessions; you have been clean and sober for a certain length of time and continue to attend AA or NA — any measures you took to put that problem behind you and make sure it will not be a factor again. Then turn the conversation back to your strengths and accomplishments, stressing what you did well in the past and that you can make it happen again.

This positive, up-front approach makes a good impression if the employer is familiar with the disease and understands, even a little, the recovery process. That good impression can be enhanced by the way you present yourself in the interview.

Too often, recovering people have such a poor self-image, particularly if they have been incarcerated, that they appear unmotivated. They need to create a new image that says, "I'm a winner! I was on top once and I'll be on top again!" That kind of image is the result of externals, such as clothing, facial expression, body positioning and movements, voice intonation, and attitude.

How you look and talk can land the job — or lose it — in the first four minutes of the interview.[2] A positive first impression carries through the entire interview, putting a "halo effect" around everything you reveal (even a prison record).

To create a winning image, you want a professional appearance: clothing that is clean, crisply pressed, well-fitting, and appropriate for the job and company; polished shoes; a friendly smile and warm handshake; and eye contact. Speak clearly, firmly, and slowly enough to make each word heard, and maintain an upright posture, as well as an attentive facial expression.

Sherwood says:

> There is no question that appearance is a big part of image, and image is a big part of the employer's hiring decision. One major problem for people who have been in prison is that cadaverous look, like they've been living in a cave. No skin color. They look dead. I recommend getting into a good physical fitness program, going to the sun room and getting a tan, working out and meeting people who are healthy, in a healthy, exercise-oriented environment, buying yourself some good-looking

clothes — then two or three days later, you look like a million bucks.

But, no matter how professional you look or how confident you sound, no employer will hire you unless you measure high on the *attitude* scale. If you convey an attitude that is bored, defensive, discouraged, resentful, or unenthusiastic, the employer won't hire you, no matter what your qualifications. The person who gets hired is the person whose attitude projects enthusiasm about his or her career, goals, and plans, as well as about the job opening and the company's objectives. Your enthusiasm will impress anyone who wants an employee who is a go-getter, even if that employee has a tainted past.

Evaluate Interview Results

After each interview, you will find a post-interview review helpful. You have tried to convey a positive image, to speak honestly about past issues, and to assess whether or not you can recover in this job with this company. Now, before you forget details of the interview, make a written review of such questions as these:

- Did you make a good impression?
- Were you prompt, friendly, and courteous?
- Were you prepared with a typed resumé, letters of recommendation, and other relevant documents?
- Did you give enough information about your qualifications to help the interviewer make a hiring decision?
- Did you forget to say something important?
- Did you stay positive?
- Did you answer every question honestly and briefly?
- Were you appropriately dressed?
- Did you speak clearly, firmly?
- Did you show enthusiasm for the job opening?
- Where did you lose control or sense that the interviewer was losing interest? How did you try to reestablish rapport?

- Why do you think you did or did not get a job offer?
- Did you ask questions about the job and the company to show your interest?
- Did you ask for advice or referrals?
- What questions did you stumble over, and how can you answer them more effectively next time? Do you need to rehearse or role-play particular interview questions?
- What else could you have done better?

By analyzing each interview, you can spot areas that consistently cause you difficulties and take steps to improve your interview skills.

❋ ❋ ❋ ❋ ❋

No one ever gave a perfect interview. There are too many variables, too many surprises, too many human foibles to contend with. When, after two or three interviews, you find the same stumbling blocks, you can focus on them, rehearse your responses, ask for suggestions from employed friends, and work on feeling more comfortable and less fearful.

Some company out there needs you. With time, persistence, and self-confidence, you will find that special place. As you gain confidence in your interview skills, these stumbling blocks can become stepping stones to the right job in the right company.

ENDNOTES
Chapter Seven

1. "The Job-Hunter's Guide," *The Executive Female* (July/August 1988): 49.
2. "The Sounds of Silence," *The Executive Female* (July/August 1988): 49.

CHAPTER EIGHT

FOR THE LICENSED PROFESSIONAL

Those who must have a license to practice — doctors, pharmacists, nurses, lawyers, veterinarians, physician's assistants, osteopaths, and dentists — can have their license suspended or revoked. Without that license, they cannot practice their profession.

When most of us get dismissed or decide to change jobs, we can choose from many possibilities; but for the licensed professional, changing a career may mean uprooting a way of life. Most of us might feel temporarily anxious or depressed because we lost our job, but the licensed professional may feel permanently disgraced and totally devastated.

Only a few years ago, once an addicted person was called before any licensing body, that professional's license would almost certainly be suspended or revoked, even if the professional went through treatment and regularly attended a support group or aftercare.

Because of these boards' punitive actions, licensed professionals have been afraid to refer themselves for treatment. Peers, partners, associates, and staff members have refused to identify addicted colleagues because they did not want to be labeled informers.[1] Instead, they covered up the other's behavior. Says a recovering operating room nurse, "People in professions cover-up and overlook a lot. Many times, I've been in the operating room and seen a doctor come in too drunk to stand up. A doctor would hold him up and walk him out, and after a while, another doctor would come in and perform the surgery. No one said anything about it." This "protect-your-own" attitude kept many professionals from getting the help they needed.

New View at the Top

About 1981, state licensing boards began to change their attitude toward drug-impaired professionals. They gradually began to favor rehabilitation instead of punishment. Today, mostly through the efforts of recovering professionals who doggedly fought for legislation and negotiated with the boards to evolve acceptable plans, virtually every state in this country has programs to assist professionals into treatment and enable them to keep their license.

Some programs, like the New Mexico Board of Pharmacy's Pharmacists Recovery Network (PRN), investigate alleged drug abuse, intervene when necessary, and monitor and support the professional through aftercare and continued recovery. Programs are operated on a voluntary basis by medical societies, as in Georgia and Ohio.[2] One program, authorized by the Colorado Board of Medical Examiners, operates a not-for-profit corporation that functions as an Employee Assistance Program. The Colorado Physician Health Program aims for early detection of drug problems, intervention, evaluation, and treatment referral *before* the physician's license is jeopardized.[3]

Each program is different and each case is handled individually. But, in general, the programs operate with similar procedures.

*1. The assistance program and/or board receives a
complaint about a licensed professional.*

That complaint may be a telephone call from a concerned
employer, spouse, friend, family member, partner, or associate;
or, it may be an irate letter from an offended patient or client. If
the board receives the complaint, it can refer the matter to the
assistance program or take action to intervene or discipline, as
the case warrants. When a law is broken, the board is required
to hold a hearing in which the professional's ability to practice
is evaluated.

Licensed professionals rarely refer themselves. Like other
addicted people, they are more likely to deny the problem,
minimize their addiction's effect on their work performance, or
think *I can handle it* or *I'm too smart to get caught*. Those few
who do self-refer can contact the program directly for help,
often with such complete confidentiality that the board never
learns the person's name.

2. Program personnel investigate.

Depending on the program's procedure, the professional may
be notified of the complaint in writing and given an opportunity
to respond. Says lawyer Jim Finnen, "Conscientious practition-
ers will respond and document their performance. If they don't,
I'll bet the underlying problem is substance abuse." Unless the
board is completely satisfied with the response, it calls a hearing
to determine if professional misconduct is involved.

Other programs authorize an intervener to investigate and
determine the truth behind the complaint. The professional's
previous employers or present associates may be contacted;
arrest records may be checked. If the person has moved from
state to state, the boards of those states may be contacted for
information on other complaints. A dossier begins to build that
either supports or discredits the complaint. If substance abuse
is confirmed, the board or program takes the next step.

3. Program personnel intervene.

A formal intervention or informal confrontation may break through the professional's denial and get him or her into a treatment program. If the professional refuses to cooperate, the board will be notified and further action, such as warning, suspension, or probation, follows.

4. An agreement is signed and anonymity assured.

In most cases, the professional must sign a contract agreeing to the terms under which the board will permit him or her to continue practicing. Those terms usually include treatment and aftercare, participation in AA or other Twelve Step support groups, and random urine testing. Other evidence of rehabilitation may be required, such as a monthly status report from an AA sponsor and/or a letter from an addiction counselor.

When an impaired professionals program intervenes, this contract, plus all correspondence, documentation, and other written material, is identified by number, not name. The board may never know the identity of the recovering person. For professionals whose reputation can be shattered by even a hint of trouble, anonymity gives reassurance for them to seek and continue treatment.

Remember Walter, the pharmacist who was convicted of a felony? When he was arrested, his employer fired him and notified the Board of Pharmacy. At that point, the Board was required to hold a hearing to ascertain whether Walter was a potential danger to the public. Meanwhile, Walter put himself into treatment and instructed his counselor to inform the Board. At the State Board hearing, Walter asked his counselor, the family therapist, his lawyer, and his AA sponsor to appear on his behalf. The Board was satisfied that Walter was well-established in his recovery and allowed him to keep his license during a five-year probationary period.

If contract terms are followed for the prescribed length of time (usually from two to five years), the professional is fully reinstated.

5. Monitoring continues during the probabtionary period.

Program staff may monitor the professional's progress through treatment and during probation. They keep track of urine tests, reports, and group attendance, and they give encouragement and support by personal contact.

In a few states, the licensing board may contract with an outside organization to perform all monitoring services. In New Mexico, the Board of Medical Examiners lobbied the legislature to raise license renewal fees ten dollars to help fund a Monitored Treatment Program (MTP) for physicians, a program that was initiated by the Physicians Aid Committee of the New Mexico Medical Society.

Once a week, the MTP brings together recovering physicians for peer confrontation and support, with an MTP counselor to facilitate discussion. They deal with recovery issues specific to physicians and other health professionals, such as rebuilding a practice, regaining the right to write prescriptions, handling lawsuits, and repairing doctor-patient relationships. This close, weekly interaction helps spot shifts in behavior, motivation, and mood that might precipitate a relapse. Weekend family programs focus on codependent issues and help the spouse and children progress in their own recovery.

In addition, the MTP encourages or mandates frequent attendance at AA meetings, and it administers membership-wide random urine testing. Says Karen Klett, MTP Executive Director,

> Urine testing documents recovery. It documents the person's clean-and-sober state. The MTP becomes an advocacy group to assist members and assure peers that the physician is drug-free. If the physician has lost hospital privileges, MTP documentation of clean urine can facilitate the re-privileging process.

Monitoring is not meant to be a punitive measure. Nevertheless, noncompliance results in *immediate* consequences, specifically, a report to the Board. This threat can often keep professionals clean and sober long enough for recovery to become a way of life and for damaged careers to be salvaged.

After Treatment, What?

Now that you have begun recovery, what can you do to keep growing, both as a professional and as a person? How can you deeply, truly enjoy your profession, its day-to-day challenges and rewards? How can you look at yourself and your work in new, healthier ways? Here are six suggestions that may help.

1. Cooperate with the people who are trying to help you.

Instead of seeing the licensing board and monitoring program as adversaries, you will feel less fear and resentment if you try to think of them as your partners, advocates, and defenders. They want the same thing you want: your participation as a fully functioning member of your professional community. In addition, they have the authority and clout to help you get back all the privileges you need to practice your profession.

A little humility is good medicine for your recovery. You can admit that you need someone to intervene with an employer, the Drug Enforcement Agency, or your partners. You can accept that you are not the perfect person you thought you were, and you can let others see the real you.

You can work on your attitude. At first your feelings of shame, grief, and loss may seem overwhelming. Even so, your ego may strike back, telling you that others don't understand. When you get to know the people who monitor you and when you stop trying to make excuses, you learn that they *do understand* because they are just like you.

2. Join a profession-specific support group.

You may be attending meetings of AA or NA and working closely with a Twelve Step sponsor. Good for you. But you may sometimes have difficulty relating to group members or talking freely about problems that affect your practice. If you feel that you need to talk to other recovering persons in the same profession, you may feel more comfortable and reassured in a profession-specific support group.

There are groups for lawyers, doctors, nurses, police officers, judges, stockbrokers, airline pilots, teachers, psychologists, and many others. Their meetings center around matters of special concern to each profession, as well as general recovery issues. They talk your language. Best of all, they know when you need to talk and they understand what you are trying to say. You can communicate. And when you start to communicate, you start to recover.

3. Take a look at ACOA (Adult Children of Alcoholics) and codependency issues.

Many professionals, particularly in the health care field, were caretakers as children. They may have taken care of an alcoholic parent or learned to feel responsible for others' welfare. Consequently, as adults, their desire to take care of others becomes a need to control other people. They may have difficulty establishing a relationship unless they can take care of the other person. Because they are always taking care of others, their own needs never get met. Underneath their addiction to a substance lie attitudes and behaviors that keep them miserable.

Says Brian Miscall, M.D., Chairman of the New Mexico Physicians Aid Committee,

> Those who don't do well in recovery haven't dealt with some underlying issues. After a few years of recovery, you need to deal with codependency and adult child issues to get long-term sobriety. It's a painful process, but if you don't do it, it can hurt your recovery. You must begin to work on these issues to get true serenity.

4. Consider modifying your goals.

As a licensed professional, you are prone to put too much pressure on yourself. You may have taken on too many patients, too many cases, too many apprentices, too many students. You may have set goals that meant you had to work too long, too hard, with too little time for yourself and your family. Perhaps your ambition drove you to win cases or build a practice or complete a course at such a pace that you felt you had to drink or use other drugs to relieve the stress.

You don't have to let your goals or your career drive you anymore. You don't have to push yourself so hard. You can accept fewer cases and spend more satisfying time on each one. You can write fewer articles and get more enjoyment from the research and writing. You can think less about money, numbers, and status and more about liking yourself and getting to know the people around you. You can learn when to stop trying to do more, better, faster, more perfectly. You can reset your goals and priorities to put yourself and your recovery *first*.

These changes in thinking and acting are usually more difficult for professionals than for other career people. You may feel that you would betray those who trust you if you eased up a little. You may feel guilty for not assuming your maximum responsibility for solving others' problems Yet, change is the essence of recovery. Recovery means putting yourself, your sobriety, and the guidance of your Higher Power ahead of anything else, even your profession. Without this change, without making a 180-degree turnaround in your thinking and acting, you will never gain the complete victory that is within your reach.

5. Help others.

Most impaired professionals programs, monitoring programs and profession-specific support groups need volunteers to act as Twelve Steppers, interveners, sponsors, speakers, or at-the-workplace monitors. You can help, even if you have only a few months of sobriety. You can start a support group if your city doesn't have one; you can lobby for a monitored treatment program; you can start a Hot Line for others who think they may have a problem with alcohol or other drugs; you can Twelve Step a stranger or invite a troubled friend to lunch and share your experience, strength, and hope.

All of these actions help you reach out to others. When you do, you benefit more than anyone else. Not only do you strengthen your own recovery, but you experience some gratitude for how far you have come.

6. *Follow your own advice.*

Professionals give plenty of advice about what to eat, how much rest to get, how to exercise, how to handle difficult personal and family problems, how to settle legal battles — in short, how their clients can take better care of all areas of their life. If that advice works for your clients, it will work for you. Try listening to the advice you give others, then ask yourself, *Is this something I should do for myself?* The answer is probably yes.

You probably need a thorough physical examination (How long has it been since you had your last exam?). You may need an accountant to reorganize your business accounts and taxes, plus a good lawyer to deal with creditors, irate ex-spouses, or pending lawsuits. You may need an understanding insurance agent, financial planner, or stockbroker to set long-term financial goals. You may need an exercise physiologist or a nutritionist to help you rebuild your body. More than likely, you need a family counselor to help improve communication and mend old hurts. Just as you would refer your clients to the appropriate persons, you can refer yourself. You can take responsibility for getting the help you need, even if you hate to admit you need it.

❋ ❋ ❋ ❋ ❋

If you are a licensed professional, you have a splendid opportunity to help other professionals get into their own recovery program. You can recognize the early behavioral changes that indicate addiction, and you can refuse to hide, cover-up, or overlook them. You can talk honestly and caringly to the other person, and you can see through the denial. You can spot signs of relapse and step in before it happens.

171

Says Dr. Miscall:

> In support group sessions, you can identify someone who is going to relapse, simply by observing his behavior. You hope to intervene before he starts using again. It can be very effective. There's nothing like a room full of recovering alcoholics and addicts who tell you the truth about what's going on with you.

Seeing through the denial, telling the truth, and being there to help — these are ways you can help as no one else can.

ENDNOTES
Chapter Eight

1. Kristine M. Lohr and Norman H. Engbring, "Institution-wide Program for Impaired Residents at a Major Teaching Hospital," *Journal of Medical Education* 63 (March 1988): 186.

2. Casper et al., "Establishment of the Colorado Physician Health Program with a Legislative Initiative," *Journal of the American Medical Association* 260:5 (5 August 1988): 673.

3. Ibid., 671.

CHAPTER NINE

WORKING YOUR PROGRAM AT WORK

"I'm all right when I'm in a meeting," says one support group member. "I get back my sense of who I am and what I need to do, and I get back my spiritual connection. But at work, when everything starts going crazy, I lose it. I get all wrapped up in everybody else's stuff, and I start to think crazy again. It really scares me."

It is scary to feel stress mounting as old thinking and behavior kicks in. It is terrifying to feel that the outside world has control over your inner peace. That is when your daily program can save your neck.

"Working your program" means taking recovery-oriented actions every day until they become ingrained to your thinking and behaving. It means applying recovery principles to difficult situations and allowing your Higher Power to work through you and in you and for you. Your trust in yourself and your Higher Power unclogs your thinking processes and lets solutions flow. Your calmness can even calm others and oil the wheels that get work done.

"Working your program" doesn't mean you will always find perfect peace in the midst of Pandemonium. It definitely doesn't mean you will never again make any mistakes. It does mean you have a way to work through problems constructively, without drinking, using, or otherwise falling back on addictive patterns.

The daily program you develop depends on your schedule, your lifestyle, your personality, your learning style, and many other individual factors. A daily program may include spiritual and program-based reading, prayer, meditation or visualization, contact with a support group, talking to a support group sponsor or friend, physical exercise, and self-examination, or some combination of the above. That may seem like a lot of activity for a busy working person to handle in one day, but it can be done if you start slowly and gradually add to, or change, your program until you have the right combination.

Here are other activities recovering persons include in their daily recovery programs.

- Listening to a recovery or inspirational tape while commuting to and from work.
- Repeating an affirmation, such as "My Higher Power is showing me how," or one of the slogans over and over, especially when troubled.
- Writing thoughts, observations, insights, and feelings in a journal.
- Working on a Step.

You may need to schedule time for these activities initially, but soon they will become so much a part of your day that you do them automatically.

PROGRAM PRINCIPLES

Working your program is different from working "the" program. "The" program means the Twelve Steps as originally written in the book, *Alcoholics Anonymous*, and now used as the foundation for all Twelve Step programs. "Working the program" means to apply one or more of the Twelve Steps or other program concepts to daily living and working.

"Working the program" may feel as if you are doing something wrong when you are actually doing something right. This feeling happens because you are changing old, familiar behaviors and uprooting comfortable patterns (even self-destructive patterns can feel reassuringly familiar). You are also asking other people to accept your new attitudes and behaviors and to examine their own values. When you practice recovery principles, no matter what your work environment is, you will find that your self-esteem and self-confidence will grow, your working relationships will become more satisfying, and your job performance will improve.

Powerlessness

The principle of powerlessness goes against every instinct for most of us. It maintains that you and I are powerless over people, places, and things; that we cannot change the way others behave or troubles happen or machines break down; that when we try to control outcomes, we forfeit our peace of mind; and that we must give up trying to power-drive our way to success and let our Higher Power take charge.

Powerlessness is perhaps the most difficult recovery principle to practice in the workplace. If you supervise others, own or manage a company, or make executive decisions, you may believe you need power to dominate or force others to carry out your orders and get the desired results. Certainly, as a supervisor, you can give instructions, make sure your subordinates have enough information to proceed, set a deadline, and check that the assignment is completed correctly. But you don't need *power* to do those things. You need authority, leadership, motivation, and influence.

Power is the same as control. When you try to control another person, even if that person works for you, you end up *being controlled*. Your mind becomes focused on that person, on changing or manipulating his or her thinking and behavior, until you lose control over your own thinking and behavior. If you have ever waited for co-workers to complete their assignments so that you could finish yours, you realize how powerless you are. They finish when they are good and ready, no matter how you beg, plead, harass, or threaten. Sometimes they purposely dawdle to punish you for pushing them too hard. And sometimes they work too fast and do such a sloppy job that it must be redone, putting you even farther behind schedule.

If you have ever planned a conference or business trip, you know how powerless you are. No matter how carefully you check every detail, someone brings the wrong handouts, one guest speaker fails to show up, airline flights are canceled or delayed, your glasses are in your other briefcase, and your best client is out of town. You have no power over these events, any more than you have power to start your car with a dead battery.

If you have worked for a school system, city government, or state or federal agency, you know the true meaning of powerlessness. Bureaucratic red tape and "don't rock the boat" thinking can keep your pet project at a standstill. You can fuss and fume about "the system" but you are powerless to change it. You can work within the system, look outside for an environment in which your creativity will be appreciated, or continue to bash your head against a brick wall. Trying to move the unmovable can hurt.

In private business, when you force others to see things your way, you shut off their input and creativity. You have only one brain working — yours. You can surround yourself with "yes men" (or women) to carry out your instructions to the letter; but your business is in danger of collapsing in the vacuum. You may have many good ideas, but you don't have *all* the ideas.

Accepting your powerlessness makes everybody happier. You do your job and you let others do theirs. You keep your attention focused on yourself, and you respect the rights of others to do their job in their own time and in their own way. You stop trying to change people. You concentrate on changing yourself.

You admit that the world and all its people are going to do exactly as they please, and you cannot change them. Further, you eventually come to the place where you do not *want* to change them. You'll want to do your job — whether it is running a large conglomerate or transplanting kidneys or checking groceries — to the best of your ability. You will leave the rest to your Higher Power. Since no one can predict results, you will leave results to your Higher Power too. When you stop trying to maneuver and manipulate people, places, and things, those mental battles end and your spirit declares peace.

Accepting your personal powerlessness — accepting others as they are and life as it is — frees your mental and physical energies to focus on your own responsibilities. This focusing almost automatically improves your job performance, with an important bonus: better interpersonal relationships.

Honesty

As a recovering person, you may look back over years of deceiving yourself and others. Perhaps you became so enmeshed in denial that you couldn't admit you were stealing or lying or conniving. You may have blamed others for "making" you act that way.

You may have been "cash-register honest." That is, you did not steal money from your company, you made sure your accounts balanced to the penny, and you gave an honest day's work for an honest day's pay (or so you believed). You may have disliked lying and liars and made bluntness part of your communication style. But honesty involves more than counting money and more than telling the bare-faced truth.

The recovery principle of honesty means looking at your *motives*, your intentions, the reasons why you do what you do. It means facing the truth about your drives, fears, impulses, emotions, expectations, and goals, even if the truth doesn't flatter you. When your words and actions are inconsistent with your motives, you are being dishonest.

For example, you might invite a co-worker to lunch to "get to know you better." But if your underlying motive is to gain inside information, you are being dishonest. If the other person senses you are being two-faced, you can make an enemy instead of an ally. Or you might recommend a subordinate for a departmental transfer/promotion. But if your real motive is to get rid of an ambitious person who threatens your position, you are being dishonest. Your dishonesty affects not only the person and the company, it also weakens your sense of integrity and your credibility with other subordinates.

Honesty isn't self-serving, cruel, or vindictive. Instead, it strives to be kind, gentle, and considerate of the other person's feelings. It should be patient, not explosive. A sudden burst of honesty in the middle of a business meeting may be completely inappropriate and cause more harm than good. Think through what you want to say, then ask yourself, *Is this the right time and place? Will honesty help or hurt this situation?* If you decide to express your honest opinion, be sure you have facts, evidence, and research to back you up, not just your "gut feeling."

Honesty requires self-examination. A nightly review of your day's activities helps spot incidents in which your motives may have been dishonest. As you identify dishonesty, you might write a sentence or two about the incident and your plans for handling it honestly next time. You might also talk to a counselor, sponsor, or recovering friend if the same incident keeps occurring. You might practice gentle honesty with a nonthreatening person and ask about his or her reaction. With yourself, you might face your motives quietly, privately, and prayerfully. Admitting to yourself what you honestly think and feel can relieve your tension and help you treat yourself and others more gently.

Acceptance

... I can find no serenity until I accept that person, place, thing, or situation — some fact of my life — exactly the way it is supposed to be at this moment.

Nothing, absolutely nothing happens in God's world by
mistake ... unless I accept life completely on life's terms,
I cannot be happy.[1]

The physician who wrote those words realized that *he* created
the turmoil in his life. He put himself into conflict with others
when he refused to accept them exactly as they were. He wanted
to change them, fix them, rearrange their priorities to align with
his, infuse them with his attitudes, and make them agree with his
opinions. As long as he kept trying to change others, he met with
resistance. When he began accepting, he found inner peace, as
well as outer harmony.

"But what about that so-and-so at work?" you ask. You do not
have to accept unacceptable behavior from yourself or anyone
else. You have a right to a compatible work environment with
people who make contributions, not problems. You can make
sure the other person understands the job requirements, communicate your instructions or opinions clearly, give training and
assistance to help the person do his or her job effectively, set
guidelines and due dates, and provide motivation and support.
That is all you can do.

If the other person doesn't complete a task, if poor attitudes
continue to disrupt the workplace, if sloppy work habits endanger the project's outcome, you have to accept the reality of those
circumstances — but you don't have to live with them. You can
look at your options, make a decision, and take action.

Acceptance helps you get along better with others because
you are no longer hassling them, fighting them, or undermining
their rights. Acceptance minimizes differences and helps you
adjust to change. Lack of acceptance (and failure to make the
necessary adjustments that come with accepting others) can
destroy your influence in the company.

Here's what happened to Jan, a successful career woman.

When her company went through a leveraged buy out,
Jan resisted the new regime's goals and management
style. She would not follow her new boss's directions

179

because, she said openly, "He's an inexperienced idiot." She found herself alone, alienated from other managers who were eager to get in step with the new philosophy. While she clung to the past, her influence waned. Finally, she was asked to resign. Accepting the reality of change, of new ownership and new leadership, would have made Jan an important part of the team, instead of an expendable reactionary.

Acceptance also helps you get along better with *yourself.* Too many people want to be smarter or more outgoing or more attractive, and they constantly regret their inadequacies. Their self-talk is an endless stream of "I should be more ..." or "Why can't I be more like. ..." Since they reject themselves, they assume others reject them. They automatically react with hurt, anger, or withdrawal. The more they react, the more they dislike themselves, and the more others turn away.

Self-acceptance breaks this sad cycle. As you accept yourself, you feel more comfortable with yourself, and others are more likely to feel more comfortable with you. Relationships improve and so does teamwork.

First Things First

This simple concept helps you set priorities and organize your time. First comes your recovery. Then you can determine what business activities need to be done, based on priorities. You can outline the stages and actions needed to complete a project, then start with the first. For example, you can analyze the market research before deciding on recommendations. Or you can arrange a class on a new word processing program before you introduce the software to your typing pool.

You can learn to list important daily activities, then number them in order of priority. As you complete each task in order, you know that you are taking care of the most important matters first. You are not allowing yourself to be sidetracked by the small stuff.

Priorities may change during the day as emergencies arise or new information becomes available. You can reprioritize as often as necessary, always putting the first thing first.

Keep it Simple

Instead of doing it bigger and better, why not seek a simple solution? Underneath every big production is a simple approach that you, and everyone else, would enjoy much more.

Not only is simplicity pleasant, it is also efficient and economical. I recently worked for a client who hired an advertising agency, a public relations team, an independent consulting firm, and a freelance copywriter to work on the same project. Any one of us could have done the job alone. Instead, personality conflicts, lack of communication, and duplication wasted our time and the client's money.

Are you unnecessarily complicating a simple decision, action, or task? Are you adding other people's responsibilities to your own? Are you getting involved in a situation that is none of your business? If you are, then look for ways to extricate yourself, to untangle all the interwoven details, and to stick to the bare essentials.

Easy Does It

Sometimes I find myself talking faster and faster, rushing from here to there, squeezing more activities into an already busy day. I suddenly realize that I am not doing anything well, and I tell myself, *Easy Does It. Slow down and get centered.* I breathe deeply to stop hyperventilating and purposely slow my steps. As my body slows down, my thoughts settle down.

Overcommitted days can get any working person stressed, and we know that stress can quickly trigger relapse. Find a way to make your work easier, to go slower, to do less, to create a system to do it more efficiently, or to delegate. Try to enjoy your work and not press so hard to finish everything on time, perfectly. Allow yourself to drift now and then. Learn to read your body signals — rapid breathing, tight stomach, fatigue, headache, ringing ears, clenched teeth, lower back pain — and to respond to those signals with stress-reducing activities. Take it easy on yourself; don't push yourself so hard. Ease your load by letting others help you.

Easy Does It — *but do it.* A times comes when you must make a decision, take action, and stop procrastinating. In recovery, you learn to trust yourself again, so that risk-taking and decision-making become less fearful. You will still make mistakes, but they need no longer start a chain of disasters. You can stop and regroup and start again. You can be kind to yourself and give yourself credit for trying. It might not have been easy, but at least you did it.

One Day at a Time

Businesses must constantly look ahead, setting goals that guide daily decisions and direct each employee's actions. Looking ahead becomes ingrained in a working person's mentality. But sometimes the future becomes more real than the present. Then the present gets less attention than it needs, and future goals cannot be reached. For instance, while a business owner focuses attention on expansion, a new product development program may fall behind the competition. Or while a salesperson works hard to land a new account, he or she may drop sales to old reliables.

Each day has its own problems and opportunities. If you attend to those and keep your attention directed at present tasks, your mind stays less cluttered and more productive. You can do what needs to be done today with assurance that you can take care of tomorrow's problems if and when they happen. Why borrow trouble? It may never come.

Each task has its beginning, middle, and end. As you end one, you can begin another. Some time-management experts advise that you save time by doing several tasks at once. But when I do more than one thing at a time, I get confused and sloppy. I don't know what I have signed, read, said, or heard. I have to do everything over again to make sure it was done correctly. "Not only One Day at a Time, but one *thing* at a time," advises my good friend Gene, a talented author. His advice works for me.

The person whose mind is scattered between past mistakes and future premonitions cannot perform effectively in the present. Single-focused concentration leads to quality job performance. And quality is one basis on which raises, promotions, and job satisfaction are earned.

AVOIDING COMMON CAREER MISTAKES

Practicing a recovery program helps you avoid mistakes. Instead of continuing attitudes and actions that sabotaged your career, now you can evaluate people and situations in a new, enlightened way. When you are unsure which direction to follow, you can pause, reflect, pray, and ask for guidance. You can remember basic principles, and you can do what is best for your recovery. If your efforts do not turn out as you hoped, you can pick yourself up and try again, without heaping a load of blame on your shoulders. You might even laugh a little at yourself and enjoy your own idiosyncrasies.

As you reflect on some of the career mistakes you have made, you can consider how you would handle those same situations if they happen again. You can rehearse recovery behaviors that will let you work them out smoothly, retaining your integrity, honesty, and humor. You will find that mistakes such as the following happen less and less frequently.

Thinking "I Can Do it Myself"

Being isolated is a sure sign of trouble. If you find yourself withdrawing, keeping secrets, or hiding out, old stinkin' thinkin' is distorting your view. If you are trying to force your decisions on others, you are not using all available human resources. You are letting your stubborn pride govern your thinking.

In recovery, you get involved with others, and you listen to and respect their views. You cooperate with co-workers and give their projects the same effort you give your own. You ask for help when you need it, from both co-workers and your Higher Power. When you allow yourself to reach out, you discover that there are soft edges around most people's hard exterior. Then you get to practice another recovery principle — gratitude. You get to thank and show appreciation to those who helped you, including your Higher Power.

Isolating yourself also shuts you off from industry contacts who can help your career, as well as support persons who can build your self-esteem. Failing to build a support system can undermine your career and your recovery. More jobs are gotten through networking (widening your circle of contacts) than any other means. It gives you access to tips and leads, research, recommendations, and most importantly, friendships among others who share your interests. These business friends can become an important part of your support system. Without this support system, isolation, self-pity, and negativism can quickly lead to relapse.

Even if you shunned others during your drinking or using days, you can begin today to create a support system that will see you through rough times. Invite your supervisor or a co-worker to lunch. Ask a business associate to play racquetball with you tomorrow morning. Attend a business conference. Volunteer to help a charitable organization. Do service work in your recovery support group. Help a sick friend.

As you reach out to others, you will find a few who touch your heart, a few whom you can trust, a few whom you truly love. These form your support system. These are the people who help keep you thinking straight and feeling good about yourself. You are unlikely to stay sober or succeed without them.

Failing to Set Attainable Goals

Goals can excite and inspire you, but they can also be frustrating. When you keep falling short, you may begin to think that you will never succeed. You may become disillusioned and suffer physical symptoms that lead to burnout, such as fatigue, irritability, and sleep disturbances.[2]

Many career people miss their goal because they imagine something vague, like starting their own business or getting promoted, without planning how they are going to accomplish it. They make a few halfhearted attempts, then give up. Or they set such a grand and glorious goal that only a superperson could achieve it. When they fail, they blame and shame themselves, settling for less than they are actually capable of achieving.

The recovering career person can set attainable goals and make an action plan for reaching them. An effective action plan details the stages and tasks needed to get you where you want to go. You can then apply your attention and energy to accomplishing those tasks, one at a time.

With recovery principles and your Higher Power as a guide, you can enjoy working toward your goals, even if you never reach them. You can adjust your expectations of yourself and others, and you can reset your goals, honestly reviewing where you want to go.

Expecting Others to Notice and Reward You

Often, in the corporate world, the hard-working, loyal, dedicated person gets stepped on by others who are climbing up the ladder. It is okay for others to be as ambitious and capable as you are, and it is okay for someone else to succeed. What is *not okay* is being so disappointed and frustrated when your efforts don't gain you the recognition you believe you deserve that your serenity and sobriety are threatened. That emotional baggage can destroy your job satisfaction and cause animosity between you and co-workers.

Recovery teaches us that we are powerless over others, including when and how others recognize our contributions. If we insist upon getting recognition from people who cannot or will not acknowledge us, then we are doomed to despair. Our solutions are:

- To enjoy what we are doing, even if nobody ever acknowledges our efforts.
- To positively affirm our value to both the project and the organization.
- To find acceptable ways within the corporate culture to announce our own success.
- To admit our need for rewards and seek an environment in which we can receive the ones we need.
- To ask for what we need. Mostly, to face the reality that corporations do not exist to satisfy our needs, but to achieve their own goals.

Therefore, we must seek satisfaction outside the corporate structure. As we seek more balanced lives, our dependence upon work as a source of recognition and reward will diminish, and we can turn to other areas of our life to provide the fulfillment we cherish.

Underestimating Your Potential, Overestimating Your Value

Sometimes, recovering people become fixated on the present and fearful of the future. They believe they cannot improve themselves or change their circumstances. They "aren't good enough" to seek a better job, undertake a bigger project, make more money, or earn more authority.

Other recovering people may demand more than they are actually worth. They see themselves as smarter, better educated, more capable, more experienced — with more know-how and sharper instincts — than their peers. They may think they are ready for a promotion, yet they fall short of meeting their present job's requirements.

One such woman, who thought she could fill a departmental management position, crashed a weekly administration meeting, hoping she could gain the attention of higher-ups. She did get attention, but not the kind she wanted. Later, she confronted her supervisor, a woman who had earned her vice presidency the hard way, and demanded that she be given a chance to prove herself. The supervisor informed her that she had already proven that she was incapable of dealing effectively with others and that, if she could not accept her subordinate status, she could leave. Outraged, the younger woman resigned that day.

Recovery urges us to look at ourselves realistically. We are neither the worst nor the best. We are human beings in progress. As we become more solidly based in our recovery, we can set our sights a little higher.

Waiting for "the Big Break"

Unexpectedly, you meet the right person or say the right thing, and your big break happens. But nothing will come of it if you have not prepared yourself thoroughly.

In recovery language, "footwork" means putting the body and mind in motion to complete your part of a task. You definitely do not sit and wait; you keep actively working until you have done all you can do. Then, when the big break happens, you are ready to take advantage of it.

An old recovery saying goes something like this: "If you want to mow the wheat, you've got to plant the seed." Whether you are looking for a new job, approaching a new client, or proving a new theorum, if you want good results, you've got to do the footwork.

Letting Little Problems Build Up

"There's one woman at work who really irritates me," said Margaret. "By the end of the day, I'm really steaming!" One person may not seem like a big problem. Neither does one disagreement, one lost sale, one harsh word, or one embarrassing incident. You may want to overlook and dismiss these little gliches, believing that you are making too much of a minor incident or that you should be able to absorb emotional bruises without wincing.

The trouble is that your unconscious doesn't forget a single unpleasant moment. Each new happening adds to the previous ones, until you build up resentment or explode in anger. For recovering persons, these negative emotions are killers.

Irritations, disappointments, and frustrations should be dealt with immediately. If you feel too upset to discuss the situation, find a time and place to settle down and think it through. You can evaluate how you contributed to the problem or decide how you will confront the other person and what you hope to accomplish. You can determine whether a third person needs to be present to help sort out each side and witness any agreements. You can decide what behavior you will accept in the future and what you will do if such behavior is repeated.

The longer you put off recognizing and dealing with a persistent irritation, the more power you give it to disrupt your work day and affect your recovery and job performance.

Perhaps you put off doing something about a situation because you dislike confrontation. You can learn to keep your remarks simple, to say what you have to say once, firmly. You can avoid impugning a person's personality ("You're so *lazy*, no wonder your sales are down") or using sweeping generalities ("You're *always* late"). You can decide to give up people-pleasing and admit that no one can get along with everyone. You can study the other person's communication style and determine the best way to present your ideas. Finally, you can practice what you want to say, even writing down a few important ideas to remember, so you feel more confident.

As long as you come into contact with people in any way, you will collide with others. However, as a recovering person, your first priority must be to settle differences and return to a peaceful state as quickly as possible.

Making Work Your Whole Life

Recovering people tend to think and act compulsively. Take away the addictive substance and other addictive behaviors can surface.

Work is addictive when it becomes your primary source of pleasure, excitement, or satisfaction; when work issues dominate your thinking; when your family or health or personal interests suffer; or when your success or failure at work equals your success or failure as a person.

Like a chemical addiction, compulsive overwork can be characterized by denial and withdrawal. When compulsive overworkers spend eighty hours a week at the office, they usually deny their behavior is unusual. When forced to take a vacation or sick leave, they may feel uneasy, guilty, or restless; returning to work brings back a feeling of well-being.

Compulsive overworkers tend to find organizations that accept and encourage their behavior. They feel comfortable around others who set high expectations and push themselves to excel. They find it easy to fall into overworking patterns set by demanding employers, and they are likely, in turn, to reprimand subordinates who cannot keep up with the pace of this work style.

Most compulsive overworkers have difficulty establishing meaningful relationships. Some experts believe they experience so much pain in relationships that they choose work as a substitute lover. Usually they lack a support system; if they burn out, no one knows or cares.

Unfortunately for recovering people, obsession with work can cause so much stress that relapse can result. Then the very things you work for — achievement, recognition, reward, self-esteem, satisfaction — become unreachable. As part of your recovery, symptoms of compulsive overwork must be recognized and treated, or your life can become unmanageable just as it was when you were using a chemical.

THE BALANCED LIFE

The lopsided life of a compulsive overworker needs balance. So does the life of anyone who becomes overly involved with one interest, such as physical fitness, religion, family responsibilities, or a relationship. Even your recovery program can throw you off balance if you give it so much time and energy that the rest of your life suffers.

A clue for me is the proportionate amount of *mental awareness* I focus on one area. If my mental awareness is disproportionately fixed on one thing (say, a financial problem or a business decision), everything else gets neglected. If my *conversation* becomes dominated by one subject (say, a difficult assignment or a new book), then I know that I am out of balance. I believe that both my mental awareness and my conversation should reflect the variety of life experiences I have during a typical day. If not, I know that I need to shift my attention to include other matters and bring back balance.

Balance, to me, is reaching my own *satisfaction level* with each area of my life, finding the point at which I am satisfied with what I am putting in and getting out. To reach that level, I must be ruthlessly honest with myself about what level of achievement will satisfy me. When I am reasonably satisfied where I am, I can comfortably let others fall behind or pass me by in search of their own satisfaction level. I don't need to feel "less-than" when I choose to level out at a certain point while others keep striving. I don't need to keep seeking more if I already have what I want. It is okay to say, "This is enough. I'm satisfied."

However, when a person is not satisfied, he or she must give that area more time, energy, and mental awareness. For example, if you have searched your heart and found that you will not be satisfied until you reach a desired position in the company, you must shift attention to that goal. But something else must get less attention. You might choose to reduce your fitness program, to withdraw from your weekend softball game, to limit social engagements, to cook less elaborate meals and rely on more convenience foods, to hire a maid service, or to spend two nights a week, instead of seven, with your children.

You have to make those kinds of choices, but your life can still be balanced, as long as you continue to give each area some minimal attention. What drives you crazy is adding another commitment on top of an already crammed schedule.

When you reach your satisfaction level, you can stop and turn your attention to something else. Or you might find that the position you wanted doesn't provide the satisfaction you were seeking. Then you need to back off, reevaluate, and do some serious soul-searching.

We all have to define for ourselves what success is, and not just in terms of our careers. We need to think about what success means in our recovery, personal and spiritual growth, health, relationships, community and religious activities, and family responsibilities. Only we know at what level we will be satisfied, and only we can say when we have reached it.

Of course, balance is not a permanent condition. It shifts and changes as new people, new situations, new ideas, and new interests come into your life. You may always feel slightly off balance as you seek new levels of satisfaction. The important thing is to keep trying, to keep making progress. You can do it. You can decide what is best for you. You have the potential to find satisfaction in every area of your life — and that is the ultimate success.

❊ ❊ ❊ ❊ ❊

In the foreword of this book, Dr. James Schaefer discusses a new core value upon which many corporations are being rebuilt. That core value says that it is okay to have problems and still work here. As this value becomes more widely accepted; as organizations shift to more ethical, people-oriented systems; and as recovering people show that healthy, functioning employees promote a healthy, functioning organization, recovering persons will become the new role models for success. In many ways, we already are.

ENDNOTES
Chapter Nine

1. "Doctor, Alcoholic, Addict," *Alcoholics Anonymous* (New York: Alcoholics Anonymous World Services, Inc., 1976), 449.

2. Robert Dato, Ph.D., "Burnout," *Update on Human Behavior* 7, No. 4 (undated): 1-2.

COMPANY CONTRACTS AND POLICIES

No matter what kind of boss supervises you, he or she must conform to company policy. You will not get fired if company contracts, policies, or union agreements cover troubled employees or if past practices have established a precedent for management procedures.

For example, a local car dealership set this precedent: Management sent five employees to treatment over a three-year period. Each kept his or her job as long as company restrictions were followed and previous behaviors were not repeated. When one employee relapsed, he or she was immediately terminated. This practice established both policy and precedent. Employees know that the president and key managers believe in the policy of treatment for alcohol and drug abusers. They know, too, that failing to follow company policy will result in termination.

Company contracts, policies, and past practices establish the rules that bosses must follow. Unfortunately, few small- or medium-sized U.S. businesses write contracts or policies that cover alcohol or drug abuse, and many allow supervisors to make arbitrary decisions. Without a contract or written policy, your boss can judge your circumstances on the basis of his or her personal opinion. Even if he or she feels inclined to provide company support, other management persons can reverse that decision.

Some companies write alcohol and other drug policies, but fail to enforce them. They put them in the new-employee orientation brochure or post them on a remote bulletin board. They fail to educate management to follow and implement policy. They never hire support staff to enforce the policy, and they never make the policy a vital part of the company's value system. Consequently, no one follows it.

Other companies set policies for users of illicit drugs, but not for alcohol abusers. They may suspend users of illicit drugs for involvement with controlled substances, but they often turn lenient when an alcohol abuser surfaces. Employees get mixed messages and few solid guidelines.

Many private companies make policies based on finding and firing abusers. They hire undercover security personnel and run a program for random urine sampling. They train supervisors to spot alcohol problems and, when they have just cause, search for bottles or other drug supplies in an employee's locker. These companies consider alcohol or other drug abuse a risk to safety for the abuser, other workers, and the public. They want to protect the public and avoid liability suits. (Note: Both public and private employers can be subject to civil suits for "negligent retention" of an employee who is allowed to continue working while intoxicated or influenced by drugs.) The rights and welfare of the troubled employee take second place to the employer's responsibility for public safety, health, and welfare.

About ten thousand private U.S. companies — including up to 80 percent of Fortune 500 companies — now have policies for the treatment and rehabilitation of employees with alcohol or other drug use problems.[1] Often these policies revolve around an Employee Assistance Program (EAP). At best, an EAP counselor acts as the recovering person's confessor, adviser, and advocate, as well as the company's policy enforcer, referral agent, monitor, troubleshooter, and mediator. At worst, he or she becomes a company spy. However, in most cases, your job is safe as long as you follow EAP policy and can document your compliance.

Seeking employee assistance cannot get you fired; failing to meet EAP guidelines can. As long as you comply, your job stays secure. Should you fail to comply, you are subject to disciplinary measures. For example, if you fail to regularly attend required support group meetings, you may be temporarily suspended without pay. If your urine sample comes out "dirty," you may be suspended without pay and benefits, fined, or terminated immediately. You should know and understand the consequences of your actions, as detailed in your union, employment, or EAP contract.

Most companies establish a policy of progressive discipline. For example, Sandia National Laboratories follows a three-stage disciplinary program. After treatment, the recovering person must adhere to strict company guidelines — including monitored attendance at AA or NA meetings, a weekly conference with an EAP counselor, and clean urine samples — or suffer the consequences. The first disciplinary stage calls for a thirty-day suspension without pay. The second stage entails a ninety-day suspension without pay, plus loss of many company benefits. The third stage is termination. On the other hand, employees who comply with company guidelines keep their job status, salary level, and promotional opportunities — guaranteed in a confidential, written contract.

Other companies follow a different disciplinary progression. They may use a written warning system before suspension or termination. These warnings document "just cause" to support the company's later actions and meet union or EAP contract requirements.

In addition to complying with your employment, union, or EAP contract, you must obey the law. Breaking the law — drinking and driving, possession of illegal substances, vehicular homicide, or assault — may result in suspension, termination, or criminal prosecution. What actions your employer takes depends on the nature of the charges, government regulations pertaining to such charges, the employee's company record, his or her present job assignment, and, finally, the potential negative publicity.

Many companies make routine computer checks of convictions. When an employee's name appears, the company's regulatory policy activates, as in this recent incident:

> An employee at a California nuclear power plant was stopped by police for driving under the influence. Court conviction brought automatic suspension of his driver's license. During the plant's routine monthly computer check of suspended licenses, his name appeared. Because of the potential danger to public safety, plant policy forbade any person convicted of DUI (Driving Under the Influence) from working around nuclear materials. The employee was immediately transferred to a less sensitive job, informed of EAP policy and treatment options, and warned that another incident would bring immediate suspension.

An employee who loses his or her driver's license may be transferred or suspended. Government employee contracts and union agreements specify which action will be taken. In private industry, when an automobile is a requirement of the job, a suspended driver's license often means termination.

Sometimes the employer makes special arrangements under special circumstances. Recently, when a hard-working lineman lost his wife and went on an alcohol binge that ended in a DWI (Driving While Intoxicated) conviction, management at the utility company realized that the incident was a one-time mistake. Instead of suspending him, they allowed him to ride as a passenger with another lineman and continue his regular duties until he regained his license.

Find out if your company or union has a policy concerning alcohol or other drug use on or off the job. Written policies will tell you (1) what constitutes unacceptable use and what substances are prohibited, (2) how abusers will be identified, (3) what disciplinary actions management can/will take, (4) what penalties will be set for off-the-job or off-job-site use that affects job performance, (5) what happens if use/abuse occurs a second or third time. This information will help you stay on the straight-and-narrow path and avoid inadvertent missteps.

KNOW YOUR LEGAL RIGHTS

By now you may be asking, "Don't I have any legal rights? What can I do to defend myself against prejudiced bosses and restrictive company policies?" You do have some legal rights, but few protections against written company policies, contracts, or past practices. As a result of a union or employment contract, certain factors can be a condition of employment, particularly in the public sector. In utility companies and large corporations, employment contracts and union agreements govern many of your individual rights. If the employer can document noncompliance with these contracts/agreements, it can execute the prescribed disciplinary measures. Your legal recourse is exactly zero.

If you signed an EAP or treatment contract, you agreed to some kind of monitored program as a condition of employment. Post-treatment care, such as an aftercare and/or a Twelve Step program, is expected. By regularly attending a support group and submitting to urine testing, you can avoid a "probable cause" situation that would jeopardize your employment.

You can safeguard your job by knowing your federal rights, guaranteed to all United States citizens under the Constitution. Specifically, the Fourth Amendment protects against unreasonable government search and seizure without a warrant issued on the basis of probable cause; the Fifth Amendment prohibits self-incrimination (giving evidence against yourself); and the Fourteenth Amendment provides for due process and equal protection (applying the law equally to all persons).

The Fourth Amendment says that no public or private employer may search you, your desk, your lunch box, your locker, or your car without a warrant. Warrants are issued only on the basis of sufficient evidence or probable cause. Without it, a judge would consider such a search "unreasonable" and would not issue a warrant. Hence, a search or seizure would be illegal.

If random drug testing can be interpreted as "self-incrimination," the Fifth Amendment may offer protection against such a practice, unless concerns for public health, safety, and welfare or national security override that right.

The Fourteenth Amendment prohibits states from depriving any person of "life, liberty, or property without due process of law." Employment is a property right. Further, any state may not "deny any person within its jurisdiction equal protection under the law." It requires that states enforce laws fairly and ensure due process (notice and a hearing) before taking away anyone's rights.

All U.S. citizens are entitled to state civil rights, prohibiting discriminatory hiring and employment practices on the basis of age, sex, race, or religion. In the private sector, these civil rights do not include recovery from alcoholism and drug addiction. Employers in the private sector may refuse to hire, promote, or retain an employee on the basis of past or present substance abuse.

In addition to an employment, union, or EAP contract and your Constitutional and civil rights, you may have other legal recourse, depending on whether you work for a government (public) or private employer.

1. Government (Public) Employees

Are you a federal employee? Do you work for a contractor to the federal government? Are you employed by a state agency, school, housing unit, or organization that receives federal funds? Then you are covered by the Rehabilitation Act of 1973 and the Comprehensive Alcohol Abuse and Alcoholism Prevention, Treatment and Rehabilitation Act of 1970.

The Rehabilitation Act prohibits employment discrimination

against handicapped persons, including drug abusers, who are able to perform their jobs. The Act applies to government employers and to private employers who accept federal grants, loans, or assistance. Employers who are subject to the Act cannot deny employment to anyone who otherwise meets the requirements of a particular job merely because that applicant is a drug abuser.[2]

A "handicapped person" has a physical or mental impairment that substantially limits one or more of that person's major life activities; has a record of such an impairment; or is regarded as having such an impairment.[3] Does that definition mean that an alcoholic or other drug abuser is handicapped and cannot be fired? No. The law does clearly say that an alcoholic or other drug abuser whose current use of alcohol or other drugs prevents such an individual from performing the duties of the job or whose employment by reason of such current alcohol or other drug abuse constitutes a direct threat to property or the safety of others is not deemed handicapped under the law.[4]

If a worker is drunk or high on the job, he or she cannot perform the duties of the job. Anyone who drives or operates company equipment while under the influence of alcohol or other drugs endangers co-workers and the public, becoming a direct threat. The threat to public safety overrides the individual employee's rights. In such cases, laws, contracts, or union agreements give little protection from transfer, suspension, or termination. However, if an employee needs time off, vacation days, or sick leave to seek treatment for alcoholism or other drug addiction, employers affected by the Rehabilitation Act must treat the problem like any other illness.

The Comprehensive Alcohol Abuse and Alcoholism Prevention, Treatment and Rehabilitation Act of 1970 defines alcoholism as "an illness requiring treatment and rehabilitation." This law urges federal agencies to establish employee alcoholism treatment programs.

Despite these legal protections, government employees (depending on their area of activity) face tough, new anti-drug policies and sanctions. If you work in an area that affects the public's health, safety, or welfare, you may be required to comply with new drug-testing procedures. For example, the United States Department of Transportation recently enacted a random drug-testing policy that affects over eight million transportation workers, including airline pilots, railroad engineers, bus drivers, and subway and commuter train engineers. Similarly, The Interior Department now requires 17,000 employees to undergo random urinalysis.[5] The Department of Defense may soon require defense contractors to begin mandatory drug testing for workers who handle classified or sensitive projects.[6] Even the Executive Office of the President now requires random drug testing of its 1,600 employees, based on the obvious threat to national security. Based on the Drug-Free Workplace Act of 1988, all contractors and grantees who receive grants from any federal agency must provide a drug-free workplace or suffer suspension or debarment. This sweeping legislation requires federal contractors and grantees to provide drug policies, establish a drug-free awareness program, and notify employees of punitive actions that can be taken against drug sale, use, or possession in the workplace.

If you believe any of your federal rights have been violated or that you have suffered harassment, mental distress, or loss of your civil rights, you may have sufficient grounds to sue a government-related employer or seek relief through a formal grievance procedure.

2. Private Employers

Working for the government gives you more legal protection than working in private industry. Private employers run their businesses "at will," and courts uphold their rights to operate their business as they see fit. What can a private employer legally do or not do?

1. Your company has the right to employ clear-headed, law-abiding, physically and mentally capable persons. It has the right to your one-hundred-percent, unimpaired work performance. It is under no obligation to hire or retain you if you are not fit to perform the requirements of your job. Even if you are their "best salesperson" or "leading scientist" or "outstanding rookie," poor work performance, excessive absenteeism, or tardiness can get you fired.

2. Your company has the duty to protect other employees and the public. It has the right to protect itself from liability suits based on "negligent retention" of impaired employees. Your company cannot knowingly keep you working at a job that you cannot perform to acceptable standards — not without setting itself up for expensive legal action.

3. The legal principle of "employment at will" still holds up in court. It maintains that a private-industry company may fire whomever it pleases, whenever it sees fit, for whatever reason it chooses. Only stipulations under a union agreement, employment contract, or employee assistance contract limit this right. An alcohol- or drug-related incident can get you fired quickly, without recourse; it's the employer's call.

4. Some state courts are beginning to impose restrictions on private employers' long-held rights. A trickle of legal decisions support the concept of "reasonable accommodation." That is, employees should be able to seek time off for treatment *without penalty.* If employees can perform their work, they should not be fired because they acknowledge a problem and seek help.

In a recent case that reached the Ohio Supreme Court, back pay was awarded to an auto-agency employee after he was fired for asking for a month's leave to attend a recovery program. The Justice maintained that the employee was protected under the state's civil rights law.[7]

You should be "reasonably accommodated" with time off to seek treatment. Your illness should receive the same company benefits that any other illness merits. Your boss should not fire you for disclosing an alcohol or drug problem. However, second- and third-time appeals will probably start progressive discipline, as they do in the National Basketball Association (NBA).

In the NBA, a player voluntarily seeking treatment for drugs receives counseling and medical treatment, at the club's expense, and is suspended until doctors determine that he is ready to rejoin the team as an active player. A player who, after previously requesting and receiving treatment for a drug problem, comes forward a second time for such treatment, is suspended without pay during the treatment. Any subsequent drug use, even if voluntarily disclosed, results in a permanent ban, which can be reviewed after two years. An appeal for review has to be approved by the NBA and the Players Association.[8]

5. *Federal contracts and most union agreements provide for "advance notice" and "due process" before disciplinary action can be taken.* Most private companies, however, can "fire at will." If you are fired or suspended without knowing the company's policy in advance, you may be entitled to a supervisory or management/union hearing before disciplinary action can be taken.

Many companies spell out their disciplinary procedures in their EAP policy. Often, this policy includes a contract between the company and the employee that details the employee's obligations and the company's probable actions.

You should not sign any document other than the standard EAP form or treatment program contract, without first conferring with your union representative, EAP counselor, or lawyer. Any boss that demands a separate, signed agreement is overstepping his or her authority and may be liable for legal action under equal employment opportunity laws. That is, if your employer singles you out for punitive actions that apply to no one else in the company, you may be unfairly discriminated against.

Generally, you should be treated in the same manner as other employees, based on the company's past practices and your civil rights.

6. *You are entitled to accuracy and confidentiality. Employers must keep the medical portion of your personnel file strictly confidential.* If you seek help through the company's EAP, you should be assured that no one outside the EAP will know, unless you grant permission for such disclosure.

Positive urine samples often mean termination. You are entitled to accurate, verified test results. If your company uses urine testing, you should be protected against false findings.

Whether public or private, your employer has the legal cards stacked against you, especially if management can document that you breached an EAP contract or performed at a below-standard or dangerous level. However, you do have rights and legal recourse. Check with your union representative, company or personal lawyer, or the Equal Employment Opportunity Commission in your state to discuss your options.

Says Cornelius "Jim" Finnen, an attorney with extensive experience in labor relations, "I advise people who feel they are being improperly treated to contact the Equal Employment Opportunity Commission in their state and have the EEOC do a general investigation to make sure the employee's rights have not been violated."

Fighting a powerful employer can mean enduring months of sleepless nights, anxiety, anger, and isolation. But it can also mean gaining self-respect, dignity, restored reputation, and a brighter future.

ENDNOTES
Appendix A

1. Paul Raeburn, "Court Weighs Alcoholism as Disease," *The Albuquerque Journal* (December 6, 1987): H1.

2. Robert T. Angarola and Judith R. Brunton, "Substance Abuse in the Workplace: Legal Implications for Corporate Actions," *Substance Abuse in the Workplace* (San Francisco: Haight Ashbury Publications, 1984), 40.

3. Charles R. Goerth, "Alcoholics and Drug Addicts Guaranteed Employers' Support Under Federal Law," *Occupational Health & Safety* 56 (1) (January 1987): 84.

4. Ibid.

5. Judith Havemann, "Death of Son Triggered Hodel's Campaign Against Drugs," *Albuquerque Journal* (19 July 1988): B8.

6. "Carlucci Drafts Firms To Fight Drug War," *Los Angeles Times* (16 June 1988): 1.

7. Goerth, "Alcoholics and Drug Addicts," 84.

8. The Associated Press, "Congressman's Plan: Ban Drug Users Permanently," *The Albuquerque Journal* (17 November 1988): C4.

APPENDIX B

APPLYING FOR INSURANCE

When you apply for an insurance policy, you must fill out an application form which usually includes a question concerning alcoholism and/or drug addiction. This information can become available to other insurance companies who belong to the National Medical Information Bureau (NMIB). Not all insurance companies belong to NMIB, but most subscribe to this industry service.

When your application reveals a medical history of alcoholism or drug addiction, your disease puts you in a "high risk" category, along with heart disease, high blood pressure, stroke, obesity, AIDS, and many other serious mental and physical conditions. Most insurance companies turn down the application of high-risk persons.

Each insurance company words its application differently. One company asks, "Within the past ten years, have you been a member of Alcoholics Anonymous or had treatment for alcoholism?" Another, "Do you presently drink or use drugs?" and "Have you ever been treated for chemical dependency?" A third, "Have you ever been treated for or ever had any known indication of excessive use of alcohol or the use of narcotics, stimulants, sedatives, or hallucinogenic drugs?"

Check the contract's wording carefully. If you can honestly answer No to these and other questions concerning serious health problems, your application will normally be accepted.

If you answer Yes, finding health insurance coverage will be almost impossible, unless you work for a large (fifty employees or more) company that provides a group health plan. Most such plans offer "no questions asked" coverage. If you work for a smaller firm, individual health questions will be asked. The insurance company might exclude you from group coverage or refuse to insure the entire group. An exception might be made for recovering persons who have been clean and sober for ten years or more.

To get the health insurance your family needs, consider finding a job that includes a group insurance package. Keep your premiums current on any existing policies you hold. If you change jobs, be sure to convert your group policy to an individual one. Conversion usually goes through automatically. Some insurance companies that advertise on television or through the mail also offer "no questions asked" plans. While these "bargain" companies may not offer the highest quality insurance, they may give you some coverage to help meet your medical needs.

Some states have enacted legislation to set up a "health insurance pool." In New Mexico, three types of high risk persons can be covered: those who have been turned down by an insurance company, those whose policy contains a rider excluding the insured person's condition, and those whose premium rates are higher than what the pool charges. New Mexico's coverage includes standard health benefits at 20 percent higher rates. Check with your state insurance commission for information on eligibility requirements, benefits, and premiums.

With all these complications, you might wonder, *Should I lie on my application?* Those who belong to a Twelve Step program, such as AA or NA, believe that honesty is essential to recovery. But taking responsibility for one's family is also essential. Ann and Todd struggled with this conflict of principles when Todd lost his corporate job and their only income came from Ann's home-based business. Ann says:

> When Todd lost his job, we had no life or health insurance. We struggled with telling the truth on the application or lying to get it. We talked to dozens of AA friends and got advice from insurance agents in the program. In the end, we chose to lie. His sponsor agreed with us. He said there was no way that Todd himself would ever benefit from this. It was for his wife and children. We should not have to suffer by not having insurance. Todd had to take care of our future. We made the decision prayerfully. We got advice. We did our research. We decided to protect our family.

But J. Marlene Hurst, President of the Central Association of Life Underwriters, warns that Ann and Todd made a potentially disastrous decision. "Todd is taking an awful chance with his family by lying," she says. Any time an insured person dies within the standard two-year contestable period, the life insurance company automatically investigates. If a lie is discovered on the application, the insurance company will cancel the policy, return premiums without interest, and withhold death benefits. Todd's family would not have gotten a dime.

Insurance companies follow similar procedures for health insurance. When a lie on a health insurance application is uncovered, the insurance company will deny the claim and rescind the policy.

Instead of lying, look for life insurance companies that accept recovering persons; many do. A number of life insurance companies, known in the industry as "substandard groups," specialize in covering high-risk persons. Their prices may run higher, but at least you have insurance. Some will accept you while you are still attending a treatment program. They may charge a higher rate and reevaluate your policy after three to five years of sobriety before issuing a standard life insurance policy.

You can get individual health insurance for your spouse and

children at standard rates, even though you yourself are not covered. Had Todd chosen this route, he would have spent more money for his own health services, but guaranteed coverage for his family. Says Hurst, "If you are simply trying to save money or get into a group program, you are manipulating the industry. You leave yourself and your family open to having your coverage canceled."

Before you make a decision, discuss your options with an understanding, knowledgeable agent.

APPENDIX C

FILING FOR BANKRUPTCY

Chapter 13

Wage earners, small-business owners, and professionals (except stock or commodities brokers) are eligible to file for Chapter 13 bankruptcy under these conditions: they have a regular income, unsecured debts that do not exceed $100,000, and secured debts that do not exceed $350,000.[1] Under Chapter 13, filers can consolidate all debts, including taxes. The filing person works out a three-year (sometimes five-year) full or partial repayment plan which is approved by the court and administered by a trustee. This procedure protects your assets, including your home and car, while easing the pressure from creditors.

Chapter 11

If your debt exceeds the limits of Chapter 13 or you are otherwise unqualified, you can file under Chapter 11 of the 1978 Bankruptcy Reform Act, which is a slightly more complex procedure. Thousands of companies have filed — nearly 68,000 since 1978 — and most have saved their businesses by taking advantage of this legal provision. Chapter 11 allows a business owner or individual to work out an agreement with creditors that extends the time for debt repayment or compromises debt. Usually, the two sides negotiate a reasonable payment schedule and restructure debt.[2] If the individual or company still cannot pay creditors, Chaper 7 of the Federal Bankruptcy Act can be used to completely liquidate.

Chapter 7

The traditional bankruptcy process clears debt by turning over all your nonexempt assets to a court-appointed trustee.[3] If you have no income or if your debt outweighs your income so significantly that you cannot support a repayment plan, this filing may be your best choice. Depending on your situation, exemption statutes allow you to protect certain assets even though you discharge debts. In addition, after your assets are liquidated and dispersed to creditors, any remaining debt is excused, except for "nondischargeable" debts such as alimony, child support, taxes, government-insured student loans, and fraudulently incurred debt.[4] If you have assets in excess of specified exemptions, filing under Chapter 11 or Chapter 13 would protect those assets more effectively.

REESTABLISHING CREDIT

Says bankruptcy lawyer Jennie Deden Behles, J.D., "Once you establish some kind of post-bankruptcy record with one firm, you can generally do it with others."

Those creditors whom you have paid regularly may not know your status and may continue to grant credit privileges. Keep making your payments and you can rebuild your credit rating.

Other ways to reestablish credit include: (1) building up a savings or checking account balance, then using that amount as collateral for a loan, (2) getting a cosigner to guarantee your debt, and (3) writing a letter to your local credit bureau to explain extenuating circumstances such as illness, injury, or theft, that contributed to the bankruptcy. This letter should be placed in your file for access by any firm to whom you make credit application.

"Logically," says Behles, "creditors should prefer to grant credit to someone who has filed bankruptcy, because once you have filed a bankruptcy, you cannot file another one for six years. Basically, you are a better credit risk. Most banks and commercial lending institutions take that point into consideration, especially in a situation where there was a good reason for the bankruptcy. If a divorce or illness or drug problem caused the disaster — but prior to that situation their credit was fine — they don't have too much trouble getting credit. They have a history of paying their bills, and now that they've done a bankruptcy, they can *afford* to pay their bills."

ENDNOTES
Appendix C

1. Mary S. Butler, "Answers to Your Most-Asked Legal Questions," *Consumer Digest* (March/April 1988): 73.

2. Walecia Konrad, "Battered but Not Broke," *Working Woman* (October 1985): 66.

3. Butler, "Answers to Your Most-Asked Legal Questions," 73.

4. Manuel Schiffres, "Wiping Clean the Slate on Debt," *U. S. News & World Report* (21 April 1986): 58.

SUGGESTED READING

Adams, John D. ed. *Transforming Work.* Alexandria, VA: Miles River Press, 1984.

Alberti, Robert E., and Michael L. Emmons. *Your Perfect Right: A Guide to Assertive Living.* San Luis Obispo, CA: Impact Publishers, 1986.

Alcoholics Anonymous. *Alcoholics Anonymous: The Story of How Many Thousands of Men and Women Have Recovered from Alcoholism. Third Edition.* New York: Alcoholics Anonymous World Services, Inc., 1976.

Allen, Jeffrey G. *How to Turn an Interview into a Job.* New York: Fireside/Simon & Schuster, 1983.

Azrin, Nathan H., and Victoria B. Besalel, *Finding a Job.* Berkeley, CA: Ten Speed Press, 1982.

Bass, Charles D. *Banishing Fear from Your Life.* New York: Bantam Books, 1986.

Beattie, Melody. *Codependent No More.* Center City, MN: Hazelden Educational Materials, 1987.

Beatty, Richard H. *The Five-Minute Interview.* New York: John Wiley & Sons, 1986.

Beatty, Richard H. *The Resumé Kit.* New York: John Wiley & Sons, 1981.

Benson, Herbert. *Beyond the Relaxation Response.* New York: Berkeley Books, 1984.

Benson, Herbert, and Miriam Klipper. *The Relaxation Response.* New York: Avon Books, 1976.

Bradshaw, John. *Healing the Shame That Binds You.* Pompano Beach, FL: Health Communications, Inc., 1988.

Bramson, R.M. *Coping with Difficult People.* New York: Doubleday, 1981.

Bramson, Robert M. *Coping with Difficult People . . . in Business and in Life.* New York: Ballantine Books, 1981.

Branden, Nathaniel. *Honoring the Self (Personal Integrity and the Heroic Potentials of Human Nature).* Boston: Houghton Mifflin Company, 1983.

Briggs, Dorothy Corkille. *Celebrate Your Self.* New York: Doubleday, 1977.

Brown, Barbara B. *New Mind, New Body Bio-Feedback: New Directions for the Mind.* Berkeley, CA: University of California Press, 1974.

Catalyst Staff. *Upward Mobility.* New York: Warner Books, 1982.

Clance, Pauline Rose. *The Impostor Phenomenon: Overcoming the Fear That Haunts Your Success.* Atlanta: Peachtree Pubs., 1985.

Cook, James R. *The Start-Up Entrepreneur.* New York: New American Library, 1986.

Crewe, Charles W. *A Look at Relapse.* Center City, MN: Hazelden Educational Materials, 1980.

Daley, Dennis C. *Relapse Prevention Workbook.* Holmes Beach, FL: Learning Publications, Inc., 1986.

Davidson, Jeffrey P. *Blow Your Own Horn — How to Market Yourself and Your Career.* AMACOM, 1987.

Davis, Martha, Elizabeth Eshelman, and Matthew McKay. *The Relaxation and Stress Reduction Workbook.* Oakland, CA: New Harbinger Publications, 1988.

Deal, Terrence E., and Allen A. Kennedy. *Corporate Cultures: The Rites and Rituals of Corporate Life.* New York: Addison-Wesley, 1982.

Dickhui, Harold W. *The Professional Resumé and Job Search Guide.* New York: Prentice Hall, 1981.

Earle, M., Dr. *Physician, Heal Thyself!* Minneapolis, MN: CompCare, 1981.

Eyre, Linda, and Richard Eyre. *Life Balance — Bringing Harmony to Your Everyday Life.* New York: Ballantine Books, 1987.

Fast, Julius. *Body Language.* New York: Pocket Books, 1970.

Figler, Howard E. *The Complete Job Search Handbook: Presenting the Skills You Need to Get Any Job, and Have a Good Time Doing It.* New York: Holt, Rinehart and Winston, 1979.

Fishel, Ruth. *Learning to Live in the Now.* Pompano Beach, FL: Health Communications, Inc., 1988.

Fournies, Ferdinand F. *Why Employees Don't Do What They're Supposed To Do — and What To Do About It.* Summit, PA: Liberty House, 1988.

Frey, William H., II., with Muriel Langseth. *Crying: The Mystery of Tears.* Minneapolis: Winston Press, 1985.

Friedman, Martha. *Overcoming the Fear of Success.* New York: Warner Books, 1980.

Gerberg, Robert J. *Robert Gerberg's Job Changing System.* Kansas City, MO: Andrews and McMeel, 1986.

Gillies, Jerry. *Money-Love.* New York: Warner Books, 1981.

Girdano, D. A., and G. S. Everly, Jr. *Controlling Stress and Tension: A Holistic Approach.* Englewood Cliffs, N.J.: Prentice-Hall, 1979.

Gold, Mark S. *The Good News About Depression.* New York: Bantam Books, 1987.

Gold, Mark S. *800-COCAINE.* Toronto: Bantam Books, 1984.

Gorski, Terence T., and Merlene Miller. *Staying Sober: A Guide for Relapse Prevention.* Independence, MO: Independence Press, 1986.

Gorski, Terence T., and Merlene Miller. *Counseling for Relapse Prevention.* Independence, MO: Independence Press, 1982.*The Phases and Warning Signs of Relapse.* Independence, MO: Herald House, Independence Press, 1984.

Grimmett, John O. *Barriers Against Recovery.* Center City, MN: Hazelden Educational Materials, 1982.

Groupe, Vincent, ed. *Alcoholism Rehabilitation: Methods and Experiences of Private Rehabilitation Centers.* New Brunswick, NJ: Rutgers Center of Alcohol Studies, 1978.

Grove, Andrew S. *One-on-One With Andy Grove: How to Manage Your Boss, Yourself, and Your Coworkers.* New York: Penguin Books, 1988.

Half, Robert. *Robert Half on Hiring.* New York: Plume/New American Library, 1985.

215

Half, Robert. *The Robert Half Way to Get Hired in Today's Job Market.* New York: Bantam Books, 1981.

Hall, Lindsey, and Leigh Cohn. *Recoveries.* Carlsbad, CA: Gurze Books, 1987.

Helmstetter, Shad. *What to Say When You Talk to Yourself.* New York: Pocket Books, 1986.

Howard, Robert. *Brave New Workplace.* New York: Penguin Books, 1986.

Hyatt, Carole, and Linda Gottlieb. *When Smart People Fail: Rebuilding Yourself for Success.* New York: Penguin Books, 1987.

Irish, Richard K. *Go Hire Yourself an Employer.* New York: Anchor Press/Doubleday, 1978.

Jackson, Tom. *The Perfect Resumé.* New York: Anchor Press/Doubleday, 1980.

Jackson, Tom. *Guerrilla Tactics in the Job Market.* New York: Bantam Books, 1980.

Jampolsky, Gerald G. *Goodbye to Guilt.* New York: Bantam Books, 1985.

Jeffers, Susan. *Feel the Fear and Do It Anyway.* New York: Fawcett Columbine, 1987.

Johnson Institute Staff. *How to Use Intervention in Your Professional Practice.* Minneapolis, MN: Johnson Institute, 1987.

Josefowitz, Natasha, and Herman Gadon. *Fitting In: How to Get a Good Start in Your New Job.* New York: Addison-Wesley, 1988.

Kaufman, Phyllis C., and Arnold Corrigan. *No Nonsense Interviewing: How to Get the Job You Want.* Stamford, CN: Longmeadow Press, 1988.

Kennedy, Marilyn Moats. *Office Politics: Seizing Power, Wielding Clout.* New York: Warner Books, 1980.

Ketcham, Katherine, and L. Ann Mueller. *Eating Right to Live Sober.* Seattle, WA: Madrona Publishers, 1981.

Kiechel, Walter, III. *Starting Over.* New York: Time, Inc., 1984.

King, Patricia. *Never Work for a Jerk!* New York: Dell Publishing, 1987.

Klantz, Pauline. *If I'm So Successful Why Do I Feel Like a Fake.* New York: Peach Tree Press, 1985.

Klaas, Joe. *The Twelve Steps to Happiness.* Center City, MN: Hazelden Educational Materials, 1982.

Krauss, Pesach, and Morrie Goldfischer. *Why Me? Coping with Grief, Loss, and Change.* New York: Bantam Books, 1988.

Land, Donald R. *Eat Right!* Center City, MN: Hazelden Educational Materials, 1985.

Lathrop, Richard. *Who's Hiring Who.* Berkeley, CA: Ten Speed Press, 1977.

Lazarus, Arnold A. *In the Mind's Eye: The Power of Imagery for Personal Enrichment.* New York: Guilford Publications, 1985.

LeBoeuf, Michal. *Working Smart — How to Accomplish More in Half the Time.* New York: Warner Books, 1979.

Lee, Wayne. *Formulating and Reaching Goals.* Champaign, IL: Research Press Company, 1978.

Mackenzie, R. Alex. *The Time Trap — How to Get More Done in Less Time.* New York: McGraw-Hill, 1972.

Marks, Edith, and Adele Lewis. *Job Hunting for the Disabled.* Woodbury, New York: Barron's Educational Series, Inc., 1983.

Marlatt, G. Alan, and Judith R. Gordon. *Relapse Prevention.* New York: The Guilford Press, 1985.

Marlatt, G. Alan, and Judith R. Gordon. *Relapse Prevention — Maintenance Strategies in the Treatment of Addictive Behaviors.* New York: Guilford Press, 1985.

Maslach, Christina. *Burnout — The Cost of Caring.* New York: Prentice Hall, 1982.

McLaughlin, John E., and Stephen K. Merman. *Writing a Job-Winning Resumé.* New York: Prentice Hall, 1986.

Medley, H. Anthony. *Sweaty Palms — The Neglected Art of Being Interviewed.* Berkeley, CA: Ten Speed Press, 1978.

Milam, James R., and Katherine Ketcham. *Under the Influence: A Guide to the Myths and Realities of Alcoholism.* Seattle: Madrona Publishers, Inc. 1981.

Milgram, Gail G., and Barbara S. McCrady. *Employee Assistance: Policies and Programs.* New Brunswick, NJ: Center of Alcohol Studies, Rutgers University, 1986.

Miller, Merlene, et al. *Learning to Live Again: A Guide for Recovery from Alcoholism.* Independence, MO: Independence Press, 1982.

Miller, Neal E., et al. *Biofeedback and Self-Control.* Chicago: Aldine Publishing Company, 1974.

Monat, Alan, and Richard S. Lazarus, eds. *Stress and Coping.* New York: Columbia University Press, 1985.

Morin, William J., and James C. Cabrera. *Parting Company.* San Diego: Harcourt Brace Jovanovich, 1984.

Mumey, Jack, and Anne S. Hatcher. *Good Food for a Sober Life.* Chicago: Contemporary Books, 1987.

Myers, Judy. *Staying Sober — A Nutrition and Exercise Program for the Recovering Alcoholic.* New York: Pocket Books, 1987.

Noble, John. *The Job Search Handbook.* Boston: Bob Adams, Inc., 1988.

Norfolk, Donald. *Executive Stress.* New York: Warner Books, 1977.

O'Connell, Kathleen R. *End of the Line: Quitting Cocaine.* Philadelphia: The Westminister Press, 1985.

Payne, Richard A. *Executive Strategies.* New York: National Institute of Business Management, 1987.

Peters, Thomas, and Robert Waterman. *In Search of Excellence: Lessons from America's Best-Run Companies.* New York: Warner Books, 1982.

Petras, Kathryn, and Ross Petras. *The Only Job Hunting Guide You'll Ever Need.* New York: Poseiden Press, 1989.

Plas, Jeanne M., and Kathleen V. Hooper-Dempsey. *Working Up a Storm.* New York: W.W. Norton & Company, 1988.

Plumez, Jacqueline Hornor, with Karla Dougherty. *Divorcing a Corporation: How to Know When — and if — a Job Change Is Right for You.* New York: Random House, 1986.

Potter, Beverly. *Preventing Job Burnout.* Los Altos, CA: Crisp Publications, Inc., 1987.

Robinson, Bryan E. *Work Addiction.* Pompano Beach, FL: Health Communications, Inc., 1989.

Rosellini, Gayle, and Mark Worden. *Of Course You're Angry.* Center City, MN: Hazelden Educational Materials, 1986.

Rosellini, Gayle, and Mark Worden. *Strong Choices, Weak Choices: The Challenge of Change in Recovery.* Center City, MN: Hazelden Educational Materials, 1988.

Schaef, Anne Wilson. *Co-Dependence: Misunderstood, Mistreated.* San Francisco: Harper & Row, 1986.

Schaef, Anne Wilson. *When Society Becomes an Addict.* San Francisco: Harper & Row, 1987.

Schuman, Nancy, and William Lewis. *Revising Your Resumé.* New York: Wiley Press, 1986.

Seymour, Richard B., and David E. Smith. *Drugfree: A Unique, Positive Approach to Staying Off Alcohol and Other Drugs.* New York: Facts On File Publications, 1987.

Sheehy, Gail. *Pathfinders.* New York: Bantam Books, 1982.

Sunshine, Linda, and John W. Wright. *The 100 Best Treatment Centers for Alcoholism and Drug Abuse.* New York: Avon Books, 1988.

Sher, Barbara. *How to Get What You REALLY Want.* New York: Ballantine Books, 1979.

Sinetar, Marsha. *Do What You Love and The Money Will Follow: Discovering Your Right Livelihood.* Paulist Press, 1987 and Critique Publishing, 1989.

Smith, Dr. David E., et al., eds. *Substance Abuse in the Workplace.* San Francisco: Haight-Ashbury Publications, 1985.

Snelling, Robert O., Sr., and Anne Snelling. *Jobs!* New York: Fireside, 1989.

Spicer, Jerry, ed. *The EAP Solution: Current Trends & Future Issues.* Center City, MN: Hazelden Educational Materials, 1987.

Steinmetz, J., et al. *Managing Stress: Before It Manages You.* Palo Alto, CA: Bull Publishing, 1980.

Stoop, Dr. David. *Self Talk: Key to Personal Growth.* Old Tappan, New Jersey: Power Books, 1982.

Tavris, Carl. *Anger: The Misunderstood Emotion.* New York: Simon & Schuster, 1984.

Wallach, Ellen J., and Peter Arnold. *The Job Search Companion: The Organizer for Job Seekers.* Boston: The Harvard Common Press, 1984.

Wehrung, Donald A., and Kenneth R. MacCrimmon. *Taking Risks: The Management of Uncertainty.* New York: The Free Press, 1986.

Weisberg, Jerry, and Gene Hawes. *Rx for Recovery: The Medical and Health Guide for Alcoholics, Addicts, and Their Families.* New York: Franklin Watts, 1988.

Welch, Mary Scott. *Networking.* New York: Warner Books, 1981.

Whitfield, Charles L. *Alcoholism and Spirituality.* Rutherford, NJ: Distributed by Thomas W. Perrin, Inc., 1985.

Winston, Stephanie. *The Organized Manager: New Ways to Manage Time, Paper and People.* New York: Warner Books, 1983.

Woititz, Janet Geringer. *Home Away From Home — The Art of Self Sabotage.* Pompano Beach, FL: Health Communications, Inc., 1987.

Wrich, J. *Employee Assistance Programs.* Center City, MN: Hazelden Educational Materials, 1974. *See also The Employee Assistance Program, Updated for the 1980's.* Center City, MN: Hazelden Educational Materials, 1980.

Wuertzer, Patricia, and Lucinda May. *Relax, Recover: Stress Management for Recovering People.* Center City, Minn.: Hazelden Educational Materials, 1988.

Wurtman, Judith J. *Managing Your Mind and Mood Through Food.* New York: Perennial Library, 1988.

Yate, Martin John. *Knock 'em Dead — With Great Answers to Tough Interview Questions.* Boston: Bob Adams, Inc., 1988.

Index

A

Acceptance, 178-180
Admission of guilt, 112-113
"A" does not equal "C" concept,
   67-68
Adult Children of Alcoholics
   (ACOA), 169
Aerobic exercise, 70
Alcoholics Anonymous, 174
Anger, 39-41
Anonymity:
   tell no one, 43-44
   tell everyone, 44-45
   tell on "need to know"
     basis, 45-47
   during interview, 156-157
Application, insurance, 205-208
Application, job, 148-149
Appearance, professional,
   160-161
Assertiveness training, 40
Attitude, 72-73, 161
Awareness, mental, 190
Awareness training, 40

B

Balanced life, 190-191
Bankruptcy, 95
   Chapter 11, 209-210
   Chapter 13, 209
   Chapter 7, 210
   reestablishing credit,
     210-211
   See also, Financial problems

Behavior:
   compulsive, 62
   overworkers, 189-190
   socially appropriate, 83
Big break, waiting for, 187
Boards, state licensing, 164

C

Caffeine, 69
Career commitment,
   reassurance of, 113
Career mistakes:
   compulsive overwork,
     189-190
   expecting to be noticed
     and rewarded by others,
     185-186
   failing to set attainable
     goals, 185
   letting little problems
     build up, 188-189
   thinking "I can do it
     myself," 183-184
   underestimating your
     potential, overestimating
     your value, 186-187
Career, new, 124-126
   changing, 119, 122
   new approach to counselors,
     120
   mistakes, 183-189
Change, gradual, 21-23
Changing jobs, 126-129
Codependency issues, 169